Blue Arabesque

Patricia Hampl

Blue
Arabesque

A SEARCH FOR THE SUBLIME

HARCOURT, INC.

ORLANDO   AUSTIN   NEW YORK

SAN DIEGO   TORONTO   LONDON

Requests for permission to make copies
of any part of the work should be submitted online at
www.harcourt.com/contact or mailed to the following address:
Permissions Department, Harcourt, Inc.,
6277 Sea Harbor Drive, Orlando, Florida 32887-6777.

www.HarcourtBooks.com

A portion of "Divan" originally appeared under the title "Pilgrim" in
Granta magazine, and later in *Best Spiritual Writing 2004;* the section of
"Camera Obscura" about Jerome Hill first appeared as "Memory's Movies"
in *Beyond Document,* an anthology of essays about nonfiction film; part of
"Balcony" was published first in *The American Scholar* where it appeared as
"Relics of St. Katherine," and later in the anthology *Re-readings.*

Library of Congress Cataloging-in-Publication Data
Blue arabesque: a search for the sublime/Patricia Hampl.

p.   cm.

1. Hampl, Patricia, Aesthetics.   2. Hampl, Patricia,
Travel—Mediterranean Region.   3. Matisse, Henri, 1869–
1954—Appreciation.   4. Poets, American—20th century—
Biography.

I. Title.

PS3558.A4575Z46   2006

818'.5409—dc22   2006004788

ISBN-13: 978-0-15-101506-1   ISBN-10: 0-15-101506-6

Text set in Spectrum
Designed by Lydia D'moch

Printed in the United States of America
First edition

C E G I K J H F D

For Terrence

I am made of all that I have seen.

—*Henri Matisse*

ONE

Cell

A spring day, 1972, best I can remember. I had taken the train from St. Paul, along the Mississippi, across green Wisconsin, to Chicago. And now, just checked into my crummy hotel, I was hurrying to meet a friend at the Chicago Art Institute, a place I didn't know. We had agreed on the museum cafeteria, and I was directed by a guard through a series of connected galleries to a staircase. I was late—of course. Rushing—of course—paying no attention to the paintings on the walls as I hurried to get where I was supposed to have been five minutes earlier.

Then, unexpectedly, several galleries shy of my destination, I came to a halt before a large, rather muddy painting in a heavy gold-colored frame, a Matisse labeled *Femme et poissons rouges,* rendered in English, *Woman Before an Aquarium.* But that's wrong: I didn't halt, didn't stop. I was stopped. Apprehended, even. That's how it felt. I stood before the painting a long minute. I couldn't move away. I couldn't have said why. I was simply fastened there.

I wasn't in the habit of being moved by art. I wasn't much of a museum goer. I'd never even taken an art history class, and I thought of myself as a person almost uniquely ungifted in the visual arts. "Patricia, dear," Sister Antoinette had said as she swished between the desks of the second graders at St. Luke's School to see what we had drawn on the construction paper she had passed out for the class frieze, "you don't need to tape yours on the blackboard with the others. You can do the lettering underneath."

I took it as a life assignment—doing the lettering underneath. Let *the others* not only make the drawings but look at the drawings. Fingerpaints, I remember dimly, had been delicious. I excelled at slinging raw color on big sheets, rubbing spirals with my fists, scraping squiggles with my nails. But I couldn't draw, couldn't *see* how to lure images from eye to hand to paper. I could only *get* things by writing them, reading them. In the beginning, truly for me, was the Word.

Maybe only someone so innocent of art history could be riveted by a picture as I was that day by Matisse's gazing woman. I had grown up in the magical realism of pre–Vatican II Catholicism, and the possibility of an ordinary person being visited by apparitions was packed into the dark kit of my mind. Bernadette in her wooden clogs picking up kindling; the Virgin appearing out of nowhere in the cleft of a rock—why not? Being spoken to by a picture? I couldn't deny it.

One way or another, ever since that uncanny moment in the Chicago Art Institute when I was searching not for art but for the cafeteria, I've been staring inwardly at that painting of the thoughtful woman who stares, in turn, at a goldfish bowl. She—*it,* the entire wordless logic of Matisse's deftly composed rectangle—became in an instant, and remained, an icon. I would have worn it around my neck like a holy scapular if the museum shop had sold such a thing.

Of course I did buy a postcard of the picture. It is propped still on my desk, as it has followed me around to all my rooms, all my desks, over the years: the woman with her no-nonsense post–Great War bob, chin resting on crossed hands, elbows propped on the peachy table where, slightly to the left, a pedestal fishbowl stands, surrounded by pinecones and a few needly branches strewn with artful carelessness. A small white rectangle rests on the table as well — a notepad. Of course: she's a writer. Eventually she will *say* something about the goldfish. Behind the woman a blue screen — Moroccan, I later learned — a prop Matisse brought back to his Nice studio from one of his North African trips. It hints at a mysterious aqua beyond.

The woman's head is about the size of the fishbowl and is on its level. Her eyes, though dark, are also fish, a sly parallelism Matisse has imposed. Her steady eyes are the same fish shape, fish size, as the orange strokes she regards from beneath the serene line of her plucked brows. The woman looks at the fish with fixed concentration or somnolent fascination or—what *is* the nature of her fishy gaze that holds in exquisite balance the paradox of passion and detachment, of intimacy and distance? I wonder still.

I absorbed the painting as something religious, but the fascination was entirely secular. Here was body-and-soul revealed in an undivided paradise of being. An adult congruence, not the cloudy unity of childhood memory. A madonna, but a modern one, "liberated," as we were saying without irony in 1972. Free, even, of eros. Not a woman being looked *at.* This woman was *doing* the looking.

But for once I wasn't thinking in words; I was hammered by the image. I couldn't explain what the picture expressed, what I intuited from it. But that it spoke, I had no doubt. I was just starting my life, fresh from university, dumb job, no "skills," outfitted only with a vexed boyfriend life, various predictable dreamy dreams, plenty of attitude. An English major on the loose at last.

I knew that the woman in the painting, whoever, whatever she was, held in the quality of her gaze the clairvoyant image of a future I wanted, a way of being in the world that it would be very good to achieve—if it could be achieved.

And what was that? What was she? A woman regarding a glass globe: in the fishbowl, several aloof residents, glinting dimly from their distorting medium, hypnotic but of no particular use. This modern woman looks, unblinking, at the impersonal floating world. Detached, private, her integrity steeped not in declarative authority but in an ancient lyric relation to the world. Something of eternity touched her. She was effortless. Or, as the deep language of my old faith would have said, she was *blessed.* That was it. Like the English major I was, I had my metaphor. Or at least I had my icon. She existed timelessly, this gazer at the golden fish suspended in their transparent medium. Who she was and what she regarded existed in the same transcendent realm.

Apparently I was already feeling the crush of time as an injury, an assault. So young, so ambitious (I was), but already squeezed and breathless, hating the just demands of schedules and duties. I worked for a radio station, editing copy, a deadline-beset existence. But I seemed to possess a memory trace, something imprinted not from my own experience but from instinct, of how life *should* be. It should be filled with the clean light of that gaze, uninterrupted. Looking and musing were the job description I sought.

Isn't that why I'd majored in English to begin with, without knowing it? Not to teach, not to be a librarian, not for a job. To be left alone to read an endless novel, looking up from time to time for whole minutes out the window, letting the story impress itself not only on my mind, but on the world out there, letting the words and world get all mixed up together. To gaze at the world and make sentences from its passing images. That was eternity, it was time as it should be, moving like clouds, the forms changing into story.

But I was beginning to see, now that I was out of school, that the world was not set up for sitting and staring, that time was no friendly giant lofting me gently into the imagination. Maybe somewhere "back there" in human history time had been, like these uncaring fish, effortlessly buoyant. That was my odd youthful nostalgia—a yearning for a state of being I'd only experienced while reading long nineteenth-century novels as a girl. It was an existence composed entirely of the mind floating unimpeded over experience. Thoughts of this sort, no doubt, are what gave rise to the belief the ancients held of the Golden Age. And goldfish, I had read somewhere, were for the ancients the emblem of that ineffable lost Golden Age. The ancients hadn't experienced their Golden Age, either—it was their moony dream, their nostalgia.

But just when did time, that diaphanous material, fray into rush? The way I imagined it, woolly minutes had once streamed across an eternity of spun-silk nanoseconds, piling up into hours that wove themselves into the voluminous yard goods of days that, in turn, got stitched into weeks and months. Wasn't that how it once was—the heavily embroidered yesteryears folded away in the scented armoires of the seasons, and consigned to the vast linen closet of the ages where the first tensile thread of our story on the planet emerged from the bobbin of history? But just *when* in all this warping and woofing—or maybe *how*—did time cease to be a treasure and turn, instead, into the fret of the drive time commute?

For moderns—for us—there is something illicit, it seems, about wasted time, the empty hours of contemplation when a thought unfurls, figures of speech budding and blossoming, articulation drifting like spent petals onto the dark table we all once gathered around to talk and talk, letting time get the better of us. *Just taking our time,* as we say. That is, letting time take us.

"Can you say," I once inquired of a sixty-year-old cloistered nun who had lived (vibrantly, it seemed) from the age of nineteen in her monastery cell, "what the core of contemplative life is?"

"Leisure," she said, without hesitation, her china blue eyes cheerfully steady on me. I suppose I expected her to say, "Prayer." Or maybe "The search for God." Or "Inner peace." Inner peace would have been good. One of the big-ticket items of spirituality.

She saw I didn't see.

"It takes time to do this," she said finally.

Her "this" being the kind of work that requires abdication from time's industrial purpose (doing things, getting things). By choosing leisure she had bid farewell to the fevered enterprise of getting-and-spending whereby, as the poet said, we lay waste our powers.

Wordsworth was wringing his Romantic hands as the Industrial Revolution revved its engines to stoke the dark Satanic mills, which Blake also regarded with Luddite despair. The English landscape—the world's—was changing forever, they knew (they grieved). So now, two centuries after Blake stood on England's green and pleasant land and Wordsworth wandered amid his daffodils, here we are writing checks to the Sierra Club, trying to bind up the wounds of modern (now postmodern) velocity, the insignia of greed.

But the raid on ease was to be more invasive, more intimate: speed attacking the very pulse of life. The eye has taken the most direct blow—and gladly. After the dark Satanic mills and the getting-and-spending, came the thrilling speed-linked frames—"the movies" we still call them. The word trails clouds of the first audience's naive wonder at sitting in the dark and watching pictures radiate not only image but rhythm. *Movies.*

Add automobiles, jets, the you-name-it-you-get-it of the latest technology, the high-speed this, and cable that, the steamy proximity of the ever-interrupting world (You've got mail!). And so it's been smashed—the long reign of slowness (and let's admit, of boredom, of tedium, of brute labor), reaching back to antiquity and forward to living memory. What's amazing—how every modern generation registers this speed with fresh dismay, as if it were the first to take the hit.

We aren't shocked, as Blake was, by the ruin of the pastoral world. We're born into a landscape that we expect to be scarred. We seem to understand we're fighting now over *what's left.*

The contemporary shock is more insidious, the lowgrade Sturm und Drang of what is now called stress. Gone, the birthright of the uninterrupted gaze. Gone, perception's voluptuous stretch. But the body, apparently, never accustoms itself to time's stampede. It gets the jitters, the mind cracks experience into jagged pieces. We become postmodern, which is to say, speedy. Maybe all that languor of yesteryear is still out there somewhere in a slag heap of antimacassars and long sentences with dependent clauses, along with all the discarded decorative stuff that junks up art and clear communication.

Or maybe that has been the point, even the project, of modernity: to abandon the gaze, to give over to the glimpse. Accept that truth is relative, authenticity is personal, and art is the business of broken bits. Admit that the fragment is our totem. And that catching things on the fly, no matter how exhausting, is more real and right than any fullness of classic form.

Even Proust, whose novel lays claim to the twentieth century's memory project more than any other, displayed a consciousness splintered and faceted. For all the page-long sentences he was still writing when Matisse painted his gazing girl, for all the invocation of "lost time," Proust's book is really a postmodern project, grasping fragments and gestures, fastening each flitting butterfly of experience to the pinboard of the page.

Anyway, gone: the long looking of slow days, the world ordered inwardly by seeing, the act of unbroken private attention that was an expression of integrity clasping imagination, making sense, making "vision." What happened to this heritage of perception? When did our autobahn existence subvert the inner rhythm beating along the pulse and risk the loss of sensation? When did we forfeit leisure? Even our food is fast.

It takes time to do this. The nun was smiling at me. Not unkindly. In fact, she looked amused. I had been shown her little cell, the cotlike bed, the child's homework table, the straight chair, the row of library books tilted against the wall. Poems by Rumi. A biography of Glenn Gould. A nun's cell. Another archaic profession, going the way, no doubt, of leech gathering and blacksmithing and the compound sentence.

I told her earlier that I was fascinated by nuns and monks. Then I said I could never be a nun. Her smile deepened, as if I'd made a little joke. At my own expense, apparently.

THAT DAY IN THE Art Institute I finally found the cafeteria, and after lunch I dragged my friend back to the picture. She didn't seem impressed. She mentioned "more important Matisses." She leaned forward to read the painting's label, nodded at the date: 1921. He had begun his odalisques by then, she said. Those were the important Matisse pictures of the period—the odalisques.

Odalisque—a word I didn't know, but I caught the sexy onomatopoetic charge radiating the languor of the seraglio. These were the exotic women—models Matisse conscripted and perhaps, rarely, loved—but above all, women he painted in rich, languid colors for ten years of the interwar period in one apartment or another above the Mediterranean.

I wanted to defer to my friend—she had a background in art history; she knew how to look at pictures. She knew "the more important Matisses." But it was impossible to defer to anything but the painting itself. It claimed authority. I had my metaphor, but my metaphor also had me.

This one, my friend said, pointing at my madonna, doesn't show his genius as a colorist the way the odalisques do.

It was true, I later realized: no striped Turkish jammies, no lounging body, no window open to the Mediterranean light, no radical palette of the south gleaming with African memories. This woman was all thoughtful northern face, a head so weighty it was propped on her arms, which were crossed upon the plain table.

The odalisques, my friend was saying, they're the mysterious ones.

"Of course," she added, "they're all a male fantasy—the harem." She said this last word with the rueful feminist smirk we had recently adopted like new spectacles that wondrously corrected our worldview.

Was it then, when she said "the harem," or only much later, looking at the postcard I brought back to St. Paul from the Chicago museum shop, that my eye began to move away from the woman's face and her fish eyes? Past the contemplative face, past the bottled world of her gaze, my eye went to the Moroccan screen and stayed there.

I suppose it was the first time I saw the *elements* of a painting, took in, without knowing the word, the *composition,* in other words, the *thought,* of a painting. Not simply the thought as of some object, but the *thinking* of the painting, the galvanizing sense of an act of cognition occurring, unfinished but decisive, right there on the canvas. The painting—maybe any painting—was only apparently static, just as, paradoxically, contemplation (the real source of this painting) is only seemingly timeless. *It takes time to do this,* the cloistered nun had said, smiling from her lockbox of inner treasures.

The picture was not, after all, only about the woman's gazing face. It belonged as much—maybe more—to the screen, to the almost effaced, easily ignored limit behind her. The blue prop that held it all together. The scrim that hid another world—and tantalizingly revealed it or at least hinted at it.

My eye traced the pattern of the screen that formed the painting's background, a hypnotic blue X/O open-work design that enclosed the woman in the drab solitude of her Western study. Matisse had hauled the subtle North African partition across the Mediterranean back to his studio in France. To build . . .

The *harem,* my art history major friend had said, laughing the fresh feminist laugh at the familiar old male leer.

I "identified" with the northern woman gazing at her aquarium. I even wrote a poem about her that became the title of my first book, a collection of poems: *Woman Before an Aquarium.* She was modern; she was nobody's harem girl. She lived safe in her thoughts. She was outside action, beyond assault of any kind from the fierce-paced world. Nevertheless, past her contemplative face that I knew to be my own, my eye strayed to the screen, to what it concealed.

I was following Matisse, his eye, his mind, *son esprit*. Behind the blue Moroccan embrasure, I too imagined—that is, desired—a chamber of silks, fantastic patterns in gorgeous disarray, scents of spice and flower, languid poses. A world unknown to the thoughtful madonna alone in her northern cell.

TWO

Window

On May 10, 1906, Henri Matisse caught the early morning train departing the French Catalan town of Perpignan where he had been visiting his wife's family for several days. He traveled west along the coast to Collioure, the town he would return to in two weeks to spend the summer with his wife, Amélie, and their three children. The summer before in Collioure he had painted the works that had just earned him the attention-getting label *wild beast* in the galleries of Paris. But on this May morning he passed by Collioure, continuing farther west along the coast to Port-Vendres. There he boarded a ferry for Algeria. After a twenty-four-hour crossing, he reached North Africa. He was thirty-six years old, and had been painting seriously for sixteen years.

When he embarked on this journey, Matisse joined a long line of French painters trailing after Delacroix who, eighty years earlier, had made this trip south that was really a passage to the East. They sought — but what was the lure? That became my question as I started to read about the man who painted the blue Moroccan screen in the picture I had come to think of as my own.

Delacroix in 1832 might go to Algeria and Morocco un-apologetically looking for what he jubilantly called the "picturesque" and the "sublime," seeking a supply of exotic subject matter. He wrote greedily from Morocco that he saw "at every step . . . ready-made paintings that would bring twenty generations of painters wealth and glory." But Matisse in 1906 was having none of this assumption of exotic transcription. So why go to Africa?

As late as 1941, when he was an old man and long famous, he could be stung by the suggestion that, in 1906 and again during longer painting trips he made to Morocco in 1912 and 1913, he had gone "just where Delacroix had gone." In his chilly reply to this remark, Matisse made it clear he went to Tangier for his own artistic reasons, simply "because it was Africa." And then added, betraying a dismissiveness that perhaps protested too much, "Delacroix was far from my mind" (*"Delacroix était loin de mon esprit"*).

By the time he was claiming this distance from Delacroix in 1941, Matisse's odalisques, his enduring subject for years, were hanging in the great museums of Europe and America and were central to some of the most discerning private collections of modern art in the world. These lounging models, draped in richly patterned fabrics (he'd been picking up swatches and remnants at market stalls all his life, even as an impoverished art student, crazy for color), are often seated upon a divan set up in his Nice studio, the low bed layered and surrounded with carpets and textiles, curtained to make an alcove. The bed appears to be a little room of its own, a cavern. The divan is presented as architecture's most intimate interior.

Matisse must have known these recumbent figures would forever link him to the great reclining female subjects of the previous century, painted by Delacroix and

Ingres. And yet—they do not. He must have counted on that, too.

For a viewer *recognizes* the Matisse odalisques in a way impossible to apprehend the figures of Delacroix and Ingres. Though these earlier works are not always earnestly ethnographic or frankly possessive fantasias of "the East" and its "mysterious" ways, the odalisques of Delacroix and Ingres remain foreign, languorous as you and I cannot hope to be. Gaze upon them and sigh.

Matisse's *Woman Before an Aquarium* led me eventually to the odalisques of Delacroix and Ingres, creamy-fleshed, their jewel colors diffused, it seemed, by the dazzled eye of their makers. The earliest of these, the *Grande Odalisque* by Ingres, she of the backward-looking gaze and famous elongated cello back extending the female curve, is duly accessorized for the harem—jewels about the head, figured scarf tied in a semiturban, peacock fan in draped hand. At the painting's edge near her naked foot, stands a hookah, dark emblem of delirium. Ingres painted this iconic female figure in 1814, the year of Napoleon's defeat and exile to Elba, Napoleon who had claimed Egypt and the world

22

of the East for France. The painting hangs now in the Louvre, one of its greatest treasures. Matisse knew it well.

I HAVE COME TO PARIS, and I stand before the *Grande Odalisque,* taking my notes as the crowds gust through the gallery. The painting takes up most of a wall. A young father bustles forward, holding his son, a boy about eight, by the hand. He positions the child front and center, and then points to the famous *dos,* bending forward, indicating the extended backbone with a swoop of his hand.

The odalisque regards us over her shoulder, me earnestly frowning back with my notebook clutched to my chest, the father claiming space to gesture expansively, the child, looking up, unblinking. The figure is unconcerned, without shame. The world of the picture is *hers,* a stylized but dead-serious blue divan-and-drapery setup, presented without irony. A picture that is a picture, claiming the territory of the wall. It is a painting obedient to the illusions of perspective, lawbreaking only in the higher service of beauty and the ruling arabesque of the line that has counted out two more vertebrae for her back than the rest of us have.

The child stares up. His face is purely absorbed as his father directs his attention to the extra vertebrae at the base of the big womby back. There is solemnity in this moment between them: this French father handing on to his boy the *patrimoine national unique* of his people. The woman inspiring the transaction looks down complacently, as if regally acknowledging that her beauty and the beached whale of her backside are the unreal real estate of their once imperial culture, replete with alien riches, passed securely from one generation to the next in this luxurious image.

Matisse's odalisques, on the other hand, their faces often casual strokes, pinkish blobs of visage, tend to be indicative rather than representative. They are tricked out in costumes pulled from a bandbox of rumpled make-believe outfits. We know they're not real. They're playing dress-up. That is, Matisse is. These figures are the opposite of exotic—in fact, they look *familiar,* their turbans and ankle bracelets are the undisguised disguise of make-believe. They do not offer rare glimpses of "the East," or illicit peekaboos into a real or imagined sultan's world with its souk's-worth of colonial loot on exhibit. They display nothing more or less than the mind of Henri Matisse.

This, oddly enough, is what makes them familiar, passing beyond the apparent foreignness of their costumes and the faux seraglio of the studio, into the arabesques of Matisse's constructions. This created, not rendered, world follows (or helps to establish) the tendency of modern art to be about the mind of the practitioner, about perception and consciousness, and not about . . . the stuff.

Yet, how essential the stuff is, how evocative and commanding. Take away the goldfish in the bowl floating upon the Moroccan prayer rug and you take away a fragment of consciousness itself. Abandon the fossil of representation that exists in the green stroke down a nose, the persimmon edge of a petal, substitute jots of pure color, abstract and dazzling—and you have lobotomized Matisse's mind, his esprit.

MATISSE'S IRRITABILITY over a reading that linked him with Delacroix was not a problem he experienced uniquely in relation to Delacroix. Matisse did not undertake his

North African journeys in order to touch the tantalizing flesh of "the other." But even more to the point, it was antithetical to the core project of his work to discover "ready-made paintings" as Delacroix had delighted in doing—or saying he was doing. How could you pretend to *find* what had to be *made*?

Matisse could admire Delacroix. In fact, he defended and invoked him throughout his life and was given to quoting Delacroix's dictum that exactitude is not truth. Delacroix, he even argued, was unfairly criticized for not painting hands, but "claws." This, Matisse told Louis Aragon, his Boswell, was not a fault but the inevitable result of being "a painter of grand scale compositions." Delacroix had to "finish off . . . the movement, the line, the curve, the arabesque that ran through his picture. He carried it to the end of his figure's arm and there he bent it over, he finished it off with a sign, you see, a sign! . . . always the same sign." This evidence of painterly logic won Matisse's admiration.

But Delacroix's imagination, he admitted with regret, "remains anecdotal, which is too bad." Matisse's judg-

ment was severe with the severity of the make-it-new or-
thodoxy of modernity. There was no excuse for vignette-
ridden art, for mere *telling.* The great masters knew better,
using humbler materials: "Rembrandt produced biblical
scenes with cheap goods from the Turkish bazaar, yet they
conveyed all his emotion." As far as Matisse was con-
cerned, Delacroix was not alone in his "anecdotal" failure:
"Tissot painted Christ's life based on every conceivable
document. He even went to Jerusalem. And yet his work
is untrue and devoid of life." Presumably because it did
not "convey all his emotion." *His* emotion. Not the emotion latent in the subject itself, but the emotion elicited
from within the artist.

A painting must depict the act of seeing, not the object
seen. Even if that object represents an entire exotic world,
it must pass through the veil of the self to be realized—to
be art. For it is the artist's fully engaged sensibility—mind/
heart/soul—that is really at stake for modernity. For all
the critical complaint about the narcissism of modern
artists, the twentieth century *demanded* self-absorption of its
great ones: Don't give us your skills, give us your attitude.

We have wanted to look not at the *thing* but at the mind beholding and rendering itself in the act of attention.

Worth a pause—for art itself is still rocking from this realization of its modern project, the weirdly spiritual (because personalized) vocation that spawned Fauvism, Cubism, Surrealism, Abstract this, Expressionist that, the masses of intervening and conflicting movements and directions that have tried to define what it means to convey, visually, *all one's emotion* in the presence of the resolutely material world.

This reliance on the self was not for Matisse mere ego (though this is the man whose wooing of his wife included the remark, "Mademoiselle, I love you dearly, but I shall always love painting more"). Matisse saw the self essentially as the maquette for the larger mystery of creation. Like Augustine, that first and greatest autobiographer, he inquired of himself in order to inquire of existence. "There are so many things I would like to understand, and most of all *myself*," Matisse wrote in a letter late in 1938, "—after a half century of hard work and reflection the wall is still there. Nature—or rather, *my nature*—remains mysterious."

No wonder Matisse's frustration at being mistaken for a disciple of Delacroix. He might have claimed just as fairly in 1941 that not only Delacroix, but Orientalism was far from his mind in Algeria in 1906, in Morocco in 1912, even in his studio above the Mediterranean where, during the interwar years, he propped up his girls, looking for all the world like a bourgeois sultan who preferred even in his imagination to stay snug at home. Was he a twentieth-century indulgent fantasist to Delacroix's nineteenth-century colonial ethnographer? Which one — or both? — is the voyeur? Does it matter?

LONG BEFORE Orientalism became an evil word, Matisse's Fauve eye was seeking an elixir in — and from — North Africa quite removed from the "ready-made" scenes that had so excited Delacroix. Yet during his two scant weeks in Algeria, Matisse dutifully followed the well-trod artist-tourist route, sketching, collecting images — the goldfish, the dizzy patterns of perspective-bashing textiles, the grave interiors of Arab cafés, the dry hills "the color of a lion's skin" as he wrote back to a friend. All the talismans that he would, in time, make his own. Yet what Matisse sought in 1906 was not, apparently, a glimpse of the swooning figures of the harem, nor the hidden life behind the screens and veils. The veil he wanted to raise was the tissue that obscured his own mind, his *nature,* as he said with enduring frustration in 1938.

Delacroix, for his part, had been positively feverish, sketching and note taking when — to his astonishment — he breached the divide of the harem in Algiers in 1832. For him the harem, the real one he believed himself to be glimpsing, *was* the thing. His "nature" was simply the gift and skill he possessed to *get it.*

He had been invited for a brief visit to the home of the associate of the chief engineer of the harbor of Algiers who, the story goes, allowed him into the harem, where the women and children of his house lived. Apparently they had been alerted to the artist's arrival. Perhaps it was a case of giving the visitor a good show. The women were all dressed up, "surrounded by mounds of silk and gold." Delacroix, according to the report of a friend, "was as if intoxicated by the spectacle he had before his eyes." He sketched frantically, noting in his sketchbook the colors of garments and furnishings ("pearl blue—black chalk—blue silk—or white?—green and white striped . . ."), even taking down the names of the women in the room—Bayah, Mouni, Zorah. . . .

This sighting resulted in the most famous of all Orientalist works, the *Femmes d'Alger dans leur appartement.* It hangs in a gallery of the Louvre not far from the *Grande Odalisque* of Ingres. Delacroix finished the painting in Paris two years after his North African trip. Two years—this pause suggests that the experience he rushed to document in his sketches and notes on the spot struck Delacroix so deeply that only time would allow its fullness to be realized.

So potent was the impression of his brief encounter with the harem, in fact, that fifteen years after his trip to Morocco, Delacroix painted a second version of the scene. Another masterpiece, but this time the lounging female figures are rendered at greater distance, more enclosed in their carpet-bedecked, tapestry-ridden world, as if given back to their privacy by the abashed owner of the earlier intrusive visit.

Delacroix's overpowering response to the harem was born in part of the singularity of his experience. He was overwhelmed by having been privileged to see what others (Occidental "others") had not seen, to penetrate the depths of the unknown. As Delacroix's friend Cournault says, the fever that seeing the harem caused him was one that "sherbets and fruits could barely appease" (cooling provisions presumed to be on hand in any seraglio). The experience was erotic. Not because Delacroix rendered the women in the soft-porn manner of many Orientalists peddling languid flesh on canvas, but erotic because of the painful ecstasy he experienced in penetrating this hidden realm.

Delacroix's women of Algiers are private, contemplative in their social setting, not sexual candy. Their apartment is no fantasy brothel. There isn't much exposed flesh, in fact. They look up, allow the instant of perception to occur, but the dark, reclusive room and all its meaning, including their draped bodies, belong to them. They are not "displayed." They remain enclosed, private. At the side, a black servant holds a curtain she will drop in a moment, taking the whole chamber away from our sight forever.

MATISSE WENT TO North Africa as a tourist, boarding a regularly scheduled ferry. Ingres didn't go at all, never traveling farther east than Rome, his harems entirely "of the mind" as Ruth Bernard Yeazell describes the lavish imaginative constructions of most Orientalists, artists and writers, few of whom "could resist describing at length what they had not seen."

But between the stay-at-home fantasy of Ingres and Matisse's frank tourism lies the arrival of Eugène Delacroix in Tangier aboard the corvette *La Perle* on January 25, 1832. Delacroix was a member of the entourage of le comte de Mornay, a diplomat sent by the French king, Louis-Philippe, to the sultan of Morocco in the face of insurrections in Oran. In a sense, Delacroix was a member of the press corps. In the earnest colonial context of the time, he had anthropological and ethnographic intentions and saw himself as responsible to history rather than to journalism. He knew he was making a voyage "that very few Christians can boast of having made," as he wrote solemnly to a friend from Tangier in 1832.

This ethnographic instinct was absent in Matisse, and perhaps his colonial (that is, possessive) eye was shut as well. Matisse thought he was making his trip in search of light, that most godlike of commodities. Actually, he was looking for *more* light, trying to ratchet up the sunshine factor that had inspired him the summer before in Collioure that had resulted in the paintings that gave him his *wild beast* badge at the 1905 Salon d'Automne.

In North Africa, Matisse sought a place where color would be even more saturated, more penetrating than it had been in Collioure. To his consternation, the powerful wattage of the desert summer was useless to this enterprise. "The light," he wrote home disconsolately, "is blinding."

He returned to Collioure which had struck him as "insipid" before he went to Algeria. But now, after the disappointment of Africa, he was glad to get home and allowed himself a sentiment worthy of a burgher: "In my slippers, I became myself again." Then, in the next sentence, the growl of the wild beast: "Painting has totally taken possession of me."

For Delacroix the experience of radical beauty in Morocco was apparently decisive. He didn't repeat it—he never returned to North Africa. Perhaps like Matisse, once back home in his slippers, he was transported from geography to the terrain of the imagination, to the act of painting itself. The overpowering experience of beauty in Morocco and Algeria during those intense months of 1832 provided Delacroix with all he needed. It had been, he said later with exquisite discretion, "a pleasure that one might well wish to experience only once in one's life."

Just so, in the fall of 1913, when Matisse was about to embark upon another much-anticipated painting trip to Tangier, he suddenly held back and decided to stay in his Paris studio. "I would probably astonish you," he wrote a friend who assumed he was off to Morocco, "if I told you that I have made plans to spend a few months in Paris . . . thinking that I had, for the time being, to engage in an effort of concentration and that the trip, the change of climate and the excitement provoked by things new, which at first touch us primarily by their picturesqueness, would lead me to dispersion."

The moral: Stay at home in your slippers.

———

THE TOURIST—that notoriously debased, denigrated bourgeois type—how easy to forget that simply *being elsewhere* is the homely version of the transcendence sought by artists. The sheer vacancy of tourism, hanging out, no job, day free to sniff around, poking into a museum in the morning, long lunch eating something weird and delicious—*friture d'anchois,* glass of white wine, humbled by a phrase book, meandering down a *borgo* toward awnings that seem to beckon, coffee at a wobbly table, world going by, the frank time-wasting of it all, eye as innocent in all this strangeness as when it first blinked upon the world—isn't that the *point* of being a person crammed into a charter flight, off to an unknown land with nothing but curiosity for an agenda? To *look.* For the goal of the tourist is the same as the artist's: to bring back pictures.

True, money is essential to travel, and tourism can be colonialism lite. The great consuming white mouth open and munching—and carefully not seeing what its contentment requires it to disregard.

Yet under the banging templates of exploitation and consumption, the magma of human desire keeps bubbling. The hunger for wonder is appeased by nothing as it is satisfied by travel. Moving around, being a stranger in a strange land, a located and limited "I" turned into an uncertain anonymous "eye," going to Paris to write about Michigan, then home to America to write about having been in Paris—this is how it is in the hunting-and-gathering civilization that is artistic endeavor.

Artists have always traveled, if only to the Louvre to copy the work of the past, entering the alien landscape of time's reversal, scratching at the door of its mysteries. So self-regarding is modernity that it tends to see everything as leading up to . . . itself. Matisse the wild beast; Picasso the iconoclast. They "break" with the past, they "change forever" the course of painting, they "lead to"—us. But in fact, they worshipped and worried over the past because that was where the evidence of greatness was displayed.

Matisse found his first encouragement for his work not in willful rebellion, but when he found a hero in the past. On a visit home to Bohain in Picardy from Paris, he and his father—the classic I-don't-get-it Dad—traveled to the provincial capital of Lille, the father to the weekly seed market, the son to see the Goyas in the museum. "He was desperate," according to his son Pierre Matisse, the legendary New York art dealer, recounting a cherished family story. "He couldn't understand the academic method, a touch of gray, then a darker tone, all their tricks and dodges—and then there was Goya. He said: 'Ah, that I can do.'"

Matisse went for years to the galleries of the Louvre, spending long hours, copying, tracing the hand of the masters, trying to get back there. He didn't wake up one morning thinking, *I don't need all this; I can paint any way I want.* As a student of the École des Beaux-Arts he knew himself to be a failure. "I believed I would never be able to paint because I didn't paint like the others," he said later in life. He could not absorb the academic technique in which "the sun of the Levant," as Pierre Schneider, the great Matisse scholar, puts it, "is drenched in the brown gravy of the École."

Travel, for an artist, wonderfully strips away professionalism, the "tricks and dodges" of the studio, the sheen of technique, the bombast of theory. The sketch is all you have, the mind's quick takes, making glancing marks in the notebook. The same applies to writers, as Henry James, in *The Art of Fiction,* says in his expansive, throat-

38

clearing way. He attests to his faith in "the rich Principle of the note": "If one was to undertake to tell tales and to report with truth on the human scene," he says, "it could but be because notes had been from the cradle the ineluctable consequence of one's greatest inward energy . . . to take them was as natural as to look, to think, to feel, to recognize, to remember."

Impossible to lug around the grand designs of ambition in the almost weightless knapsack of first perceptions. Delacroix, too, set great store in the sketch: he felt a painter should be able to finish a drawing of a man falling from a building's fifth story before the man hit the ground.

Perhaps this affirms a core belief in classical technique, but it sounds modern — catching reality on the fly, being present in the glimpse, the fleeting instant. But *getting* it. The artist as tourist is the artist freed of the fuss, fuss, fix, fix, touch of gray, then a darker tone. It is not only the exotic subjects — the women lounging on their divans, the hills the color of a lion's skin — that thrill the eye of the touring painter. The hand is enchanted, too, liberated from the easel, loosed to crayon, chalk, the pencil's smudge. The writer freed of plot, "character development," "narrative arc," hand roving over the notebook page in sentence fragments, broken images, the butterflies of observation pinned down, the bright flowers of attention pressed between the damp pages.

Religion, that other ancient enterprise of the imagination, is magnetized by travel as well. Even defined by it. Islam marks its start from migration—the original great march from Medina to Mecca. This hajj, repeated as a form of religious confirmation every year, is one of the five pillars of Islam. Not to mention the forty years of desert wandering that established Judaism, and the homeless meandering of Jesus: "Foxes have holes and the birds of the air have nests, but the Son of man has nowhere to lay his head." Pilgrimage, which is a form of tourism, reaffirms humanity's most ancient metaphor—that life is a journey. We must keep moving, it seems. The imagination is not a domestic animal. It roams, it picks up scraps where it can. A piece of paper, a stub of pencil.

Matisse came to see the airplane as the ultimate means of transport, "the flying carpet of *The Thousand and One Nights*," as he put it. To him, flight was tourism absolute—

abstracted from effort, without the earnestness of pilgrimage—experience without episode, an entirely lyric journey, pure form, travel as the float of sheer verticality. After a flight from London to Paris that astonished him, he wrote, "You find yourself in a completely white landscape, in radiant but not blinding light." Not the unhelpful "blinding light" of Algeria in 1906, but the timeless radiance of air, the very thing that had originally caused him to take the ferry to North Africa to begin with: light.

"The forms of the clouds are extremely pleasant," he says, a nineteenth-century man for whom a plane ride is magical. "Vast plains heightened by plumes of clouds seem to block the route. We come closer and then penetrate them in silent fog and diffused light. We emerge, the noise of the plane grows louder and once again we find ourselves abruptly in the bright, caressing light (a light not only bright but delectable)."

The whole experience was revelatory. "A plane trip," he said, as of a different state of being, "can help us both to forget and to find the peace of mind which makes everything possible. What is surprising is the feeling of motionlessness and of great security. It seems impossible that we could fall." He had ascended into light, his enduring subject.

A man given to discoveries—of light, color, shape— he discovered flight, which was not wholly or even essentially physical to him, when, as an old man, he experienced this miracle only imagined and dreamed of in the Golden Age. "Shouldn't one complete a young man's education," he wrote lavishly after this flight, "by sending him on a world tour, mostly by plane?"

Travel, maybe especially the surface ease of tourism, promotes the art of the sketch, of the note, forms that retain the pulse of the eye that beholds, the hand that transcribes, the intimate self that absorbs and then renders. Travel alerts the eye and humbles the hand. Its final destination is radiance: to be transported, as the mystics say. The world's transparent window finally opens wide. And the subject sketched in the notebook—goldfish, Moroccan screen, a father gesturing to his boy before a painting of a languorous woman in a gallery of the Louvre as another woman takes it down—all of it is not subject. It is window; it is eye.

THREE

Divan

*D*oesn't everything start at home? Especially the desire to escape it. Then, having escaped, to live in a permanent elegy, drawing from the well of your own hard-hearted ambition and proud rejections all the refused tendernesses, all the provincial complacencies you determined to abandon. And did abandon.

All my heroes—my saints, as I think of them—have been traitors, one way or another, to their homeplace: Matisse fleeing the priest-ridden north; Scott Fitzgerald shrugging off his (and my) likewise Catholic St. Paul; Katherine Mansfield abandoning Edwardian New Zealand

43

for the London literary life. All of them were drawn at some key point, as if by divining rod, past their initial flight, to the aquamarine rim of the Mediterranean, to the sun and the ancient source of Western culture. They sought, if unconsciously, the place where it all began. "It" being nothing less than civilization, the human impulse that organizes itself to express what it means to exist, face torched by the sun, ear filled with the rhythm of the waves, eye gorging on the gallons of light that gush over the lavender fields of Provence.

This sun-and-civilization was not Matisse's birthright. He was born on the last day of 1869 in Picardy, bordering Flanders, in northeastern France, near Van Gogh country. Sugar beet land, the hardscrabble Minnesota/North Dakota of France. A dour provincial world. Just a month before his birth the Suez Canal opened for commercial traffic, one of the signal events of nineteenth-century empire and colonial marketeering. With its opening, the Orient, the Levant, all the treasure-lands of the East drew nearer.

The new canal was a variation on the Progress/Transportation theme that had echoes elsewhere. Earlier the same year the first transcontinental railroad was completed in the United States, linking east and west. (Which would not have been cause for celebration for Delacroix who before his death in 1863 remarked, "Soon we shall be unable to go five miles without coming across those fiendish contraptions, railway trains.") In these historic linkages—grand canals and continental railroads—nineteenth-century colonialism gestures toward postmodern globalism, the culmination to which its raw spirit aspired.

Matisse grew up not only on the border of Flanders, but on the raw edge of this industrialism. The air of his boyhood town, Bohain, was grimed; the streets ran with effluent from factories that, in a generation, changed a centuries-old village of home jacquard weavers into a town of day laborers at big factories. Blake's dark Satanic mills sucked up the lives of his neighbors, men, women, and children who worked twelve hours a day in the beet-processing refineries and the textile mills of the town with a single fifteen-minute break. Belching smokestacks punctuated a landscape once marked by windmills and steeples.

There was also political humiliation: As a boy, Matisse experienced the occupation of his town by the Germans, following the mortifying French defeat of 1871. This shame occasioned an impassioned invitation from the Catholic archbishop of Algiers (formerly bishop of Nancy). "Christian people . . . now on the roads of France, of Switzerland and Belgium, fleeing your burning homes, your devastated fields," the Archbishop writes in an ecclesiastic letter, "Algeria, African France, by my Bishop's voice, opens its doors and offers you its arm. Here you will find for yourselves, your children and your families, abundant lands, more fertile than those that you left behind in the hands of the invader." In other words, overcome the humiliation of the invader by becoming the invader yourself.

Yet for all the bleak misery of Bohain, luxury was its chief occupation, beauty the business surrounding Matisse as he grew up. Bohain supplied the great couture houses of Paris with the stuff of fantasy: the gossamer fabrics shot with threaded gold, fine linens and patterned wool challis, handwoven velvets, filmy tulles and voiles, vividly dyed silks, watered and figured, cream-heavy and feathery-frail. The many textile factories of the town were almost all devoted to the high fashion and furnishing houses of Paris. "Picardy, thanks to Bohain," according to an admiring government inspector in an 1897 report, "leads the whole of France and indeed the rest of the world, in the fashion field."

Matisse never forgot that he was a provincial of the north—the cold, gray, hard-bitten, unforgiving Catholic north. Toward the end of his life, while he was working on the chapel at Vence in sunny Provence, Matisse told the movie star Edward G. Robinson, who was one of his collectors, "I've always worked like a drunken brute trying to kick the door down." Spoken like the boy still smarting from provincial humiliations, determined to crash the party. That is, the galleries.

When the time came to break away from home, Matisse did not stop at Paris, where of course ambition required him to migrate. As soon as he had some money in his pocket (actually, before he had any), he kept going south, to the sun, to the light. Years later, as an old man long resident in Nice, he still sounded like an escapee from winter as only a northlander can: "When it became clear to me," he said, "that I would see this light every morning, I could not believe my bliss." It was a grand inner homecoming to the "great dazzlement" (*"mon grand émer-veillement"*) he had felt at his first sight of the Mediterranean in 1898. You would think he had discovered the sun. In a way, he had. The sun *in* things, not just the sun falling upon them.

"NICE IS ALL DÉCOR, a very beautiful, fragile town but a town without people, without depth," Matisse wrote of the city he chose as his main residence for the rest of his life. It became his odalisque capital. But maybe Nice, a place that was "all décor," "without people," and especially "without depth," answered perfectly the description of the real estate he required.

Here, in rented rooms and apartments between 1917 and 1929, he decorated his elaborate hotel-harems as stage sets for the most intimate paintings of his long working life. But are these draped and undraped houris really "intimate"? Debate has rocked back and forth concerning the value and purpose of Matisse's preoccupation with the hieratic figures he propped up in the bewildering visual cross-purposes of his wallpapered and carpeted, striped and beflowered pocket Edens. The little moment in the Chicago Art Institute when my art history major friend told me the odalisques were "the really important paintings" and then laughed her knowing feminist laugh about the harem—this was only one of the political minefields Matisse's girls had to endure as they lounged through the century.

Are these works a signal of mere indulgence, nothing more substantial than "decoration"? A kind of regression and retreat? Or do they display a radical passion, a fever for color and body and sensuous life (the East) as against tone and intellect and rational thought (the West)? Are they bold or bourgeois? Aggressive or passive? The work of genius or a retreat from greatness? Voyeuristic or contemplative? Imperially possessive or revelatory visions of the act of seeing, the poetry of pure attention?

Long ago I succumbed to Matisse and his studio project. I've shadowed him—and his odalisques—from museum to museum in my travels since that day at the Chicago Art Institute when I gazed at the woman gazing at the goldfish. I've stalked his girls as if they had secret intelligence about the life of the mind. That's the odd part—that these luscious bodies would suggest to me "the life of the mind." Gallery after gallery, over the years, I've made my pilgrimage to these sightings of the cool-eyed woman with her faux exoticism, my stack of museum shop postcards growing like a boy's deck of baseball cards.

In Paris, great troves of Matisse girls, of course. In Nice yet more. In Baltimore I discovered the amazing cache of loungers, harried by their flowered wallpapers and Moorish screens, in the Cone Collection at the Baltimore Museum of Art. They had been collected by two sisters, Dr. Claribel and Miss Etta Cone, inspired pack rats of modern art, virtuosos of avidity. They collected everything, it seems—including, like Matisse, textiles. "I am beginning the buying all over again," Dr. Claribel writes to a friend with dismay at her own passion. "How the saris wind themselves about my heart. 'Throat' would be better, for they strangle out all other impulses. . . . Now that I stop to reason about it, it is silly foolishness, this collecting of things. But it must have some solid foundation—some foundation deep in the hearts of people. . . . It is the craving for beauty that is such a vital function of the human soul."

I even find a Matisse odalisque near home, in Minneapolis—the *Odalisque with Bowl of Fruit* (1925). The Minneapolis odalisque sits cross-legged, one bare foot crushing a carpet rose, her chemise open to the waist, her ripe breasts demurely covered with a filigree of embroidery, her eyes boldly set ahead. The odalisque face, typically, is composed of several sure strokes, and looks straight out from a looping, zigzagging environment, not a dreamy face at all, but almost stalwart, at attention. The odalisque as stern sensualist. Maybe that's why I persist in thinking these figures convey something about the life of the mind even as their breasts loll, and their patterned world swirls about them, and everything seems to invite indolence and ease. They suggest not languor but the act of perception, the self meeting the world—looking at it, as the world looks back from the vast neutrality of its material wealth.

I go to the galleries; I stand before the paintings ranked on the walls. I buy the postcards in the museum shops. Over the years my deck of cards rises. I'm a two-bit Claribel Cone, caught up in this modest "silly foolishness." The odalisques even have their own desk drawer. Occasionally, I mount a small show for myself, propping a few cards against the lamp and along the raised edge of my desk. Sometimes I do a group show, positioning Ingres's *Grande Odalisque* off to the side, Delacroix's Algerian women facing. Manet's *Olympia,* purchased after standing in line outside the Musée d'Orsay in a whipping rain for over an hour, is on display too, her insolent mouth wiping away the Giaconda smile that ruled Western art for centuries, replacing it with knowing contempt, the breathtaking smirk of a woman who knows her price.

Claribel Cone thought of collecting as a killer—the beautiful saris *strangle out* everything else, she said. She had a point. Collecting is not a simple matter of possessing. It's a way of looking: a looking that is itself a kind of craving. To look this way is to be possessed, lost.

Some of my cards are soft, almost frayed at the edges, dog-eared like a book handled over and over.

Matisse was forty-seven in 1916 when he first settled in Nice. He devoted more than a decade of his prime years to his odalisque, his "silly foolishness," to use Claribel Cone's exasperated term. Between 1919 and 1929, the count comes to about fifty major canvases of harem girls, not to mention countless preliminary drawings, sketches, vignette details. Even his artist friends thought it extreme. There's a famous photograph of Pierre Bonnard, a close friend of these years, roguishly mocking Matisse's single-mindedness. In the photo Bonnard appears fully clothed in a three-piece suit lying on Matisse's studio couch before a patterned drapery and a vase of flowers, his booted leg crossed and raised in a mock-odalisque gesture. His face in profile bears the neutral calm of the Matisse harem.

Matisse employed a series of professional models to play his odalisques, if by "professional" is meant young women, often foreign and displaced, who had no easy way of making a living and who drifted as extras and walk-ons into the early makeshift movie studios around Nice. Here, about the same time, Scott Fitzgerald's visiting American movie people in *Tender Is the Night* mingled their new fame and wealth shyly and then more boldly, and finally fatally, with the older American leisure class in residence on the Riviera. These children of Fitzgerald's Midwestern robber barons, who had linked the continent with railroads, lounged, thanks to their trust funds, on the "bright tan prayer rug of a beach" on the Côte d'Azur. The moment Dick Diver—hapless name—falls for the starlet Rosemary Speers—pitiless name—serves as well as anything as the moment when celebrity culture takes the American dream hostage, apparently forever. The moment when pop culture first claimed the ascendancy it now so fully possesses.

Matisse's models often belonged to the margins of this world. They were, in effect, actresses. These young women entered and expanded his fantasy, offering him poses, conferring about costuming and furnishings, firing the psychological atmosphere of the paintings. Of these women none was more important to the odalisque enterprise than Henriette Darricarrère who incarnated Matisse's harem world for seven years, from 1920 to 1927.

Henriette was not a refugee, not a girl alone and unprotected. She was the daughter of parents who moved from Dunkirk, where she was born in 1901, to Nice with their children who included, besides their pretty daughter, two younger sons. Henriette was drawn to performance, and was posing as a ballerina for the film cameras at the Studios de la Victorine when Matisse first observed her. In a twist on the Schwab's drugstore story, she was discovered *in* the movies rather than *for* them. She seems never to have looked back, and served Matisse faithfully as muse and fellow fantasist until she married in 1927 and left his employ. Her own daughter later posed for Matisse.

There seems to have been no love affair, in case that comes to mind—how can it not? It appears that Matisse was something of an uncle-figure. Her family remarked with approval that Matisse encouraged her piano and violin and ballet lessons, even "allowing her time" to paint and attend social events. This overall time-ownership ("allowing" her free time) suggests the link was intense, profound, not just a job with an hourly wage. So does the fact that she quit the work at the time of her marriage, as if no matter how virginal the work of modeling, she could not, as a wife, continue to participate in the fantasy it required.

Henriette was the model for the famous *Decorative Figure on an Ornamental Background* of 1925–26, where she reigns in semiprofile with regal calm amid battling decorative motifs, her swirling world anchored by a bowl of lemons at the side. She sits in an anti-Ingres ramrod position just as improbable in its straight edge as the *Grande Odalisque* is with her supine extra vertebrae.

But this is just one of many languid reclining seminudes below an open window or (less often) closed up in a fiercely decorated chamber, the moist *niçois* air cloying the room, the grit of modernity coming in from the boardwalk below. I shuffle through my deck of cards, I page through the art history books I have also collected, my eye passing over ballooning Turkish pants, running down medallions of ferocious wallpaper, on to a carelessly exposed bosom, past a finely shrouded face, one after another, these ripe fruits. I collect them all, which is to say, I love them all.

As surely Matisse did. But not a single figure commends itself as "the one," not even Henriette as the *Decorative Figure.* There is no odalisque supreme, it seems. No Matisse figure who *does* for him what the *Grande Odalisque* did for Ingres or the *Algerian Women* did for Delacroix— epitomized it all. Matisse's girls, all the rooms and divans, the wallpaper and patterns, are variations, inevitably incomplete, part of a larger idea or desire. They are a collection. And therefore rely on each other to approximate the idea of a whole.

No single odalisque compels my attention and completes my search. I find myself returning, instead, to a grainy snapshot that seems to turn up in all the art history books and biographies, dated imprecisely from the mid-1920s, when Matisse was working with Henriette at 1, place Charles-Félix in his third-floor studio.

The photograph is black-and-white, of course. This in itself makes the now-familiar Matisse-designed harem more arrestingly foreign, as if it weren't, after all, a pretend home theater, or an artist's color laboratory, but a postcard photograph snapped behind the closed door of the women's quarters. The dark-haired beauty, not Henriette but an Italian model named Zita he used only briefly, is tucked into the recess of her bower-of-textile-bliss divan, one leg raised to display an ankle bracelet, her kohl-eyed gaze directing the focus of the picture to—the artist himself.

For there is Matisse at the left, in his suit and tie, jarringly *not* part of this harem dream, slightly lower on the picture plane than Zita on her divan but larger than she because he is in the foreground, holding his drawing tablet on his knee, right hand in midstroke. He brings to mind Freud, perched at the side of the couch, dressed impeccably as a doctor in his clinic, ready to take his diagnostic notes, a painting shrink.

Even the divan is much the same as Freud's Berggasse consulting couch that went into exile with him when he was forced from Vienna to Hampstead in 1938. Like that couch, Matisse's divan is a draped daybed covered with Persian rugs and the higher math of intricately woven tapestry. The divan upon which the mind and its secrets were opened to view in the twentieth century.

But Matisse is not really drawing. He's posing. He looks straight at the camera, obediently having his picture taken. And therefore cannot know what we, regarding the picture, know: that his odalisque is taking an illicit look at him as he is being framed by the photographer. Her body dutifully holds its draped Matisse extension, but her eyes are on the loose, hungrily taking in her boss who, for once, is not looking at her.

A strange moment. Zita's mouth teeters on the verge-of-smile but does not quite fall into pleasure. The barest amusement as she turns her eyes, not her head, as if now he were caught, if only for an instant, as she is always caught. But there is—I've taken a magnifying glass to her face—something closer to worry passing across her features. Not fear, I think—she's not afraid of him. But worry of some sort. That they have been interrupted? That the photographer is taking too long? That the fragile border of their fantasy has been breached by a stranger?

Or is it—and I give over to this thought—that she feels a surprising empathy that perhaps only a model could feel. It is an abashed look, a kind of protopity, a brief solidarity that he has been reduced, as she is daily, to a pose.

AND WHAT OF my own excursions to the East?—the reen-actment of the search for the exotic, the other, or what-ever it's called now. A week into the Friendship Tour of Israel with a brief detour to Petra in Jordan and I asked to be taken to a hospital. I was possibly dying, and I thought I should say so.

Our guide, roaming the hotel to round up his charges for the morning tour, looked down where I had flung myself on a low padded bench against a wall in the pretentious lobby, and laughed out loud. Hooted. Then he turned and walked away, down the desert-colored marble corridor that swam with ominous gold light.

I had been stricken suddenly. The day before we had "done" Masada, stopping first to float in the creepy buoyancy of the Dead Sea. Then back on the bus, passing Qumran but not stopping to see the caves where, in 1947, Bedouin shepherd boys looking for a stray goat had found the Dead Sea Scrolls rolled up in ancient amphoras. I had walked without trouble to the top of the Masada citadel, surveyed Herod's realm in the fierce high wind, and readily imagined the Roman armies advancing mercilessly across the terrible openness of the plain as our guide described, feelingly, the mass suicide of the Jewish forces as they faced certain Roman victory. This is the landscape, I thought, that gave religion God "out of the whirlwind." God *as* whirlwind.

Then, as we all stared out stung, as our guide intended, with elegiac sentiments, he murmured, as if it were a minor footnote of no great matter, that "the historians" now dispute the suicide story. A legend, he said airily, but a beautiful one, yes? Then, his usual gesture—a finger tapping his gold wristwatch on his upraised arm—we must get back down to the bus.

Later, at the hotel, drinks on the terrace as the setting sun turned the baked gold of East Jerusalem sweetly pink. Everything we looked at from the Hilton on King David Street was ancient except for the hotel, built to mimic the old stone. And of course ourselves, sitting with our vodka tonics.

But then, without warning, this swoon just after breakfast. My eyes ached all along the optic nerve; my body was no longer in my possession. Waves of nausea hit and slammed. I held the sides of the bench so I wouldn't be pitched overboard, swept off in a stream of murky gold liquid that was—I could still make the connection with part of my mind—also the floor of the lobby of the Jerusalem Hilton. I closed my eyes and turned to the wall like an old peasant in a hut whose time has come.

Our guide, who had told us he had fought in the Six Days' War and who had a wry leathery face I had liked until our last exchange, returned. He touched my shoulder. He held out a can of Sprite. "Drink this," he said. He made me sit up, which I thought was extremely unwise.

Then he was gone, but other people, members of our "friendship mission" gathered around. They too urged the Sprite on me, and then, apparently reassured, one by one they left for the bus, though two women I had been avoiding during the trip for complex reasons I could no longer recall, stayed behind. They sat down wonderfully close, one on either side of me, stationed like abutments holding up the wobbly span that was me. I drank the Sprite. They, too, insisted. I mentioned again the hospital—and realized with shame that I was whimpering.

Oh no, no hospital, I was told with a pat, though neither one of the women laughed, thank God, the way the veteran of the Six Days' War had laughed.

These women I had not liked assured me I wasn't dying. They spoke with the same brisk certainty they had used several days earlier when, over drinks on the Hilton terrace with its heart-stopping views of the everlasting hills of the Old City, they had attested stoutly to their atheism as to a matter of basic hygiene. Culture—yes, they had said. But religion? A ruinous mixture of nonsense and trouble. Evil, one had said.

Now, hips snug against my own, they displayed an unmistakable lack of alarm about my situation, drifting away from my desperation to chat about the day's itinerary. We were going to Caesarea, we would see the Roman aqueduct. A good lunch was promised. I sipped the Sprite, peevishly thinking, *Nobody takes me seriously. Story of my life.*

I was dehydrated, one of the women was saying. It was not serious. It *could* be serious. But it wasn't. Not yet. Finish the Sprite.

I tried to explain that I wasn't thirsty, that I couldn't be dehydrated. I indicated my water bottle. We all drank prodigious quantities of water. This is a desert, remember, we kept telling each other.

"Electrolytes," the heavier woman said. "Your electrolytes are out of whack. It happens in the desert." She was a financial officer for a museum but spoke as one accustomed to sandstorms, camels, dry blowing nights, though all of us were from Minnesota where the license plates read LAND OF 10,000 LAKES.

She went somewhere and came back with another Sprite. She snapped open the can and handed it to me. As I raised it to drink, the sweet fizz of carbonation sprayed my face, and a brilliant collision of ecstasy and shame struck me as my mind and my body, lost lovers, found each other again in an instant. I saw in a saving flash that I had been wrong, that the war veteran tour guide was right and the two kindly atheists were right. I wasn't dying. Feeling the grainy champagne of Sprite spark through me, I was distinctly not dying. I was becoming, once again, that thing I call "myself."

PERHAPS THE SHOCK OF disorientation with its tincture of fear renewed my spirit on this guided trip through Israel and as far as Petra in Jordan. "What gives value to travel," Camus said, "is fear." And like most people, I prefer to think of myself as an independent traveler, not given to group tours. Yet I had gladly joined, when invited, this busload of American Midwestern "community leaders and artists" (the two categories being understood as mutually exclusive). A junket to the ancient place, stage set of history and myth I had grown up calling, from years of Catholic schooling, the Holy Land.

It was about two years before the second—and still current—intifada, and I think all of us on our big bus felt safe, safe enough to have come in the first place. It was still possible to see "incidents" as separate, widely spaced, unlikely. We didn't talk about our safety. We discussed the politics of the region as if everything were either in the past (violent, impossible) or somewhere in the future (hopeful, though indistinct). None of us really knew anything about it.

We had been toured around Israel and Jordan with stops at opposing camps for the past week. The Palestinian mayor of Bethlehem gave us sweet dense coffee in minute, intricately patterned cups passed from a brass tray in a serene second-floor office where a ceiling fan whirled slowly as if in a scene from *Casablanca*. He seemed to think we were influential in some way, and he gave us more time than any of the Israeli officials did, speaking with great courtesy, without bitterness, appealing to our better selves as he described the situation.

The American Israeli householder we visited later in his weirdly bland air-conditioned split-level in the subdivision, which he insisted on calling a settlement, handed around a huge container of Coke with plastic cups. Out the window of his American-style house, we could see, in the lower distance, a fenced area where Palestinian families were camping in a kind of shantytown of tarps and sagging cardboard.

Camels and SUVs, the persimmon walls of Petra, the depressing vacancy of emotion I felt at the Church of the Holy Sepulchre, the groaning buffet tables of the Israeli hotels, the conservative Catholic op-ed page writer from Minneapolis who said loudly to the Holocaust survivor before we were taken to tour Yad Vashem, "I'm not going along if this is intended to make me feel guilty."

Group tourism, in other words. By the time I collapsed in the Hilton lobby, I had reached a stress point of crabbiness, a sense of being held hostage by our handlers, a feeling of being . . . well, a tourist. Worse, a functionary in the middle-management of culture, greedy hands across the cultural divide. Why had I come? I was furious with my-self for going on this freebie junket, my paw held out for experience, a gluttony like any other.

Tourism, that dishonored if massively indulged mod-ern habit, bears its voyeuristic taint with a shrug. We all want to go ... elsewhere. We all want to see ... what's there. Much has been written in recent years about the toxic nature of "the gaze"—the man staring boldly at the woman, the vacationing rich gawking at the local-color poor, the unfair advantage of being the observer.

Yet what does the world come to if *to look,* that once un-abashed gesture, is understood to be an evil? Even Adam and Eve were allowed to gaze at the Tree and its fruit, after all. They were even instructed to *enjoy* it—an object to be regarded, if not touched or tasted. The world's first mu-seum moment, if we'd just left it at that. But who ever just leaves it? We keep reaching, eating up the world.

That afternoon, after our handlers had returned us from our round of gawking in Caesarea, the gentle atheist who had gone for the second Sprite and had given me back my life, invited me to go with her while everyone else napped. She wanted to visit the souk in East Jerusalem.

Perhaps to shake my sour antisocial feeling, perhaps because I was still wary of being alone, I went along, trotting beside her purposeful self like a good pet.

Her appetite for our trip was still lively, lacking my fussy annoyance, and the souk was an easy walk from the hotel. She had a camera, a fancy one she had been wielding the past week wherever we went. A person with an eye sharp for detail, her curiosity buoyant and benign. I could tag along with her, could maybe silence my inner grumble, and rise again to the occasion of travel, the pure act of looking. In any case, I was still a little wobbly, and she was my angel.

There was the feeling of *entering* the souk, as if the narrow streets constituted a sort of crumbling ancestral house, the streets being in effect corridors leading to chambers that were somehow secretly attached, all belonging to one large, breathing self, an organism of architecture. Passageways along the open stalls gave way here and there to a little coffee shop embedded like a fossil under a building's arch. The market radiated a satisfying paradox as if permanence and flimsiness met in an eternal congruence that held everything mysteriously together.

It was deeply satisfying to walk along the passageways, taking in the ancient buildings where people still lived in dark, cavelike apartments cool from age, not air-conditioning, the collapsible-looking market stalls on the ground floor spilling into the walkways, their corrugated roofs sloping, creating dusky interiors, produce and wares piled along the common hallways of the streets.

We allowed ourselves to get lost, reassured by the landscape of fruits and vegetables, the sharp sniff of coffee, the dust of sugar from the sweets on display, milled chickpeas, baskets of speckled beans, lacquered olives in stone vats. Narrow shops displayed bright woven fabrics—a heavily embroidered gown that seemed to contain all of Araby and flimsy silks lofting in the breeze like delicate soutanes. Clothes of the desert.

A double row of Palestinian men carried aloft a dark shape on a pallet—a body on the way to burial: they turned between two buildings and were gone with their wrapped package held above their heads. We saw—I did anyway—smiles gleaming behind the display tables, eyes sizing us up: no sale to these hotel dwellers. But mostly it was a refreshing nonhuman moment, just the vegetables and us, the pleasure of passing along the brilliant stalls as if through a pure element without any meaning beyond the delight of color.

Then my companion came to a halt, seized by the display of a spice merchant. We were in the densest part of the souk, surrounded by stalls before us and behind us, the passageway turning to yet more mounds and baskets. But this was *the picture* for her. She asked me to hold her bag for a moment while she snapped it. "I just have to get all this color," she said. And it was wonderful—the deep saturated dye of turmeric, a hypnotic yellow having nothing to do with the sun, belonging entirely to the mineral earth, sumac crushed to powder like pulverized red wine, baskets of color so intense they were delicious already, just looking at them. She put her face close to the fragrant surface, drawing in scents.

I reached for her bag as she had instructed. As I bent down I saw the face of the boy standing behind the tableful of spices. He could not have been more than twelve. I felt my own face begin to move into its let's-be-friends tourist smile—*your spices are beautiful.* My companion lifted the heavy camera to her pale face, aimed down at the palette of color. The boy was shaking his head, saying something, frowning. He was becoming agitated. It took me a moment to understand he didn't want her to take the photograph. She saw nothing, her head down and focused on what she had framed.

It happened fast. Which is to say slowly, in the endless way of moments that will be inscribed in memory. The boy said something harsh, turned to me, finding no hope of getting the attention of the woman taking the picture. He said something again, hissed across the dazzling table of his wares. Then he spit. A sharp, targeted bullet of projectile fury. It hit me sharp in the eye, exactly where he intended, I think. His own eye was dark, radiant with hatred.

He did not turn away, did not look abashed. Calm descended. I knew with that uncanny knowing of real experience, *Ah, so this is why I came — for this.* Real travel wants to be dangerous, wants to smoke out the truth of the other — providing of course you get out alive.

I put my hand to my face, astonished, my fingers damp with his thick wrath.

———

So it is possible to take what doesn't belong to you—just with a glance, a look. But like all appetites too ferocious to be explained away as a fascination with "the exotic," Matisse's attraction to the decorative arts—all those madly patterned "Eastern" draperies and harem costumes—was primal, homebound, a *donnée* for him. His father came from a line of weavers but rose to own a general store and eventually became a successful seed merchant. His mother was a milliner whose hats, people recognized, had a certain something. (Matisse married a hatmaker in his turn.) Following the fashion of the age—but with unusual finesse—his mother later took up porcelain painting. Matisse claimed he got his color sense from her. The economy of his home and of his town was predicated on the flummery of ornament and the appetite for the unnecessary. Decoration was, paradoxically, essential.

In the foul streets of Bohain, Matisse first beheld not the beautiful but the gorgeous. The liberated delight of color, the *delectable* quality of pattern was his birthright. He was surrounded by leftover beauties, snippets and patterns, bales of woven wealth on their way to other people's lives. Labor was literally woven into beauty as he first perceived it.

Cézanne was his man. "When color is at its richest," Cézanne said, "form is at its fullest." And where to find this saturation, this richness? Good counsel came from Gauguin: "O painters who are looking for a color technique, study rugs. You will find all the necessary knowledge there." Not just any rugs: "Always have the Persians in mind," he added. Even earlier, Delacroix famously made the same judgment: "The most beautiful pictures I have ever seen are some Oriental rugs."

This would have been confirmation, not news, to Matisse who lived among those who concocted the dazzling fields of silk and wool that swirled around the hourglass figures of the fashionistas of the age and swept across the furnishing fabrics of the best design houses of Paris. These colors and patterns swirled first from the hands of the workers and designers of the Bohain textile mills. Home was the workshop of the exotic. The source of the glorious was here in the northern mud, a worker's dream— and livelihood.

By the spring of 1903, after several years in Paris, Matisse's early dreams of earning fame as a painter had been shattered. He had returned in financial desperation to Bohain with his wife and three children, and later admitted he "practically decided" to "give up painting altogether." His plan was to take a job as a colorist in a rug factory. Designers were in demand, and the pay was good. In fact, Matisse's first art school had not been the École des Beaux-Arts in Paris, but a provincial night school for the sons of weavers. Even in Paris he had prudently enrolled for a diploma at the École des Arts Décoratifs. The business of ornamentation, he knew, could pay the bills.

Yet this was a young man possessed by painting. His biographer, Hilary Spurling, has found a sketch of an iris he doodled in the margin of a legal document in the law office where his father first apprenticed him. He may have been possessed by painting, but his iris isn't the wistful sketch of a repressed artist nailed to his scrivener's stool. He was practicing the decorative craft. His iris is not "in nature" but is a wholly decorative object, its natural ground not the earth, but a carpet, a scarf, a textile.

And cut flowers, the stuff of hybridization and home

gardens, are not wild, not "natural," but decorative. Horticulture and rug making, botany and Persian carpets—these crafts shelter under the same umbrella, the vulnerable, ornamental corner of human endeavor given over to what only appears to be decoration. This desire for the riches of decoration is not trivial, but as inevitable as the recurring human ache for a God in his heaven.

Matisse's first artistic allegiance was to the paradisal surface of the decorative crafts of his northern factory town. The flat floral fields of textiles were all about him—and Eden, after all, was not a mountain eyrie, not a seaside vista: it was an enclosed garden, a flat surface patterned with flowers. And not wholly utilitarian—Genesis puts us in the Garden, not on the Farm.

Upon the earthly plane of fabric, color and form display themselves without the forced hierarchy of perspective, on a democratic level, joyous floral designs of stacked-up millefleurs tapestries, and now, unfurling from the Bohain mills, the minutely twisted gold and silver gossamer of industrial fiber. These were—what else?—pictures.

And they were luxury. The textile mills of Bohain might be exploitative factories feeding the refined tastes of the Parisian design houses, but they laid out a banquet of promise to the masses as well. During his life—and long after his death—Matisse was routinely dismissed for displaying a "decorative" sensibility and for indulging his relish for loveliness. In this, he suffered the slight that women often suffer from a love of beauty, of domestic pleasures and "touches."

It didn't help that he was his own theorist, eager to explain himself, and that he wrote a lot about his artistic philosophy, thus encouraging rebuttal, rather than cannily cultivating an artistic mystique. In an oft-quoted (against him) testimony from "Notes of a Painter," his first published essay (1908), he says his dream "is an art of balance, of purity and serenity, devoid of troubling or depressing subject matter, an art that could be . . . a soothing, calming influence on the mind, something like a good armchair that provides relaxation from fatigue."

Oh-oh. How to nail yourself as unrepentantly bourgeois, a virtual philistine, in one sentence. The remark followed him the length of his long life and beyond. Never mind that earlier in the same essay he speaks of his attempt, when working with the model, to achieve "the deep gravity that persists in every human being."

Yet he did not misspeak when he enshrined the armchair and invoked relief from fatigue. His dream of beauty was in solidarity not with the idle rich but with the exhausted working poor. Only one who had seen the unforgiving circumstances of industrial labor could understand that the odalisque does not loll on her divan as an erotic opportunity but is even more deeply sensual, an image of pure leisure, that commodity most cruelly denied the poor of the earth.

Yet even to my contemplative nun leisure was essential to her monastic business, her mystical day job. And she was pledged not only to obedience and chastity, but also to poverty.

Matisse was on the side of the decorative, the frankly made-up, the brilliant and luscious. I must be, too, having sucked in my first draft of beauty also from the indulgences of life in my father's greenhouse in St. Paul, the big glass houses of geraniums, the walk-in iceboxes (as they are still called) where the cut flowers waited in tubs for funerals and weddings. It was all beauty for its own sake, for the show of it. For much of my girlhood, Memorial Day was still called, especially by older people, Decoration Day, and it was understood that the most solemn fact of life—that we die—is best honored by ornamentation.

Is that what drew me to Matisse and not to Picasso, his great rival? I felt the deep taproot of the decorative instinct in Matisse as I could not in Picasso. Yes, the *deep* root of decoration, for the surface of decoration gives way, for those who live close to its truth, to the labor and the pride in the labor that Matisse knew in the Bohain textile mills and that my father and the old Austrian growers knew at the greenhouse, their backs humped over from lifting flats of petunias, their hands cracked from tamping down the dirt around a seedling's squiggle of white root. They were the ones with real taste, my father always insisted. They could *judge.*

Matisse had faith that color was substance, not surface. It was a lyric faith, a belief not proved, but affirmed. Probably he was born with it, raised in its midst. This was not the gloomy northern Catholic stranglehold he rebelled against, but the enduring faith of his town, his hatmaking, porcelain-painting mother, his long line of weaver ancestors. He held to it.

Matisse subscribed to the old democratic weavers' definition of the decorative arts as "something more precious than wealth, within everyone's reach." The poor in spirit could hope to inherit, if not the earth, then at least a length of paradise in a bright factory-made cloth ingeniously imprinted with "a pocket jungle." He may have dressed like a bourgeois in his tweed suit and vest, but Matisse was a working boy who saw early how the lavish hungers of the rich were sated with exotic beauty, and he perceived the power of unnecessary pleasures. His harsh northern, priest-crushed Catholicism, the careful clawing for a perch on the ladder up and out of scarcity that was his father's lot—all this did not engender a bourgeois complacency. It made him a *Fauve,* a wild beast.

Matisse stood like a lightning rod between the sumptuous aesthetic of the rich that demanded the fabrics of Bohain and the proud craft of the laborers of the muddy town who provided the objects that, alone, connected the two worlds. Beauty was business; it was food and shelter. In such a hierarchical world, a world in which beauty rules daily labor and provides the very bread on the table, poverty cannot be untouched by the glories it is consigned to create. It seems Matisse never forgot that the hunger of the poor is, as the old union hymn has it, for bread—and roses.

FOUR

Camera Obscura

Directly above the glass houses of my father's greenhouse in St. Paul you could see the bulging sunroom of the Louis Hill mansion, your eye drawn irresistibly from the lowlands of the old immigrant houses where my family lived up to the nineteenth-century architectural fantasias of Summit Avenue. The Louis Hill house filled the bluff property adjoining the brownstone citadel of his father, James J. Hill. But Louis Hill's house was no castle keep like the Empire Builder's. It was a rosy confection of fine patina brick and ivory pillars, a gracious porte cochere at the front, large arched windows all around. Not the stronghold of a king, but an indulged prince's graceful pleasure palace.

The houses of father and son, side by side, presented contrary images, an architecture of oppositions. Two generations—two American centuries—were set shoulder to shoulder, at deep stylistic odds with each other, facing Summit Avenue with their visual argument. The Empire Builder's nineteenth-century pile bespoke the lonely kingliness of monstrous success, the sacerdotal nature of great American wealth. Gloom and doom and righteousness. The poor boy's astonishment at *making it* had somehow to be manacled to the earth, and James J. Hill's sooty brownstone was an abode above the abyss, a fortress hulked over the Schmidt brewery where my Uncle Frank had died in a freak industrial accident in 1936 and where the little Czech immigrant houses with their tidy survivalist vegetable gardens still endured. All that was the underworld, the world you had escaped or eluded if you had achieved Summit—"Crest Avenue," as Scott Fitzgerald called it in a short story.

Next door to the Empire Builder's gloomy grandeur, Louis Hill's mansion was a great meringue. It suggested wit, elegance. Its laugh chimed all the way to the bank, and it carried its grandeur lightly as if placed upon the earth in the dancing slippers of the well brought up and well turned out. Someone said Queen Marie of Romania had done the Charleston there at a party on the third-floor ballroom during the twenties. Of course there was a ballroom. You sensed it even without having been inside.

Yet, during my girlhood in the sixties, both houses had met the same fate: each had come into the possession of the Catholic Church. The Archdiocese had long ago inherited the Empire Builder's house. This had a certain geographic logic because the cathedral was right across the street from the dark mansion. Catholic Charities—or was it the tribunal on marriage annulments or the Legion of Decency or perhaps all of these fiefdoms of righteous morality?—had piled typewriters and tall gray file cabinets into the big parlors, along with bulky desks and the other drab paraphernalia of canon bureaucracy, leaving long, negligent scrape marks on the bald wood. Some areas were covered with linoleum.

The spacious woody rooms were crowded with mimeo machines and partitioned work spaces, metal desks slammed against mahogany paneling. A central stairway that looked eerily like the grand staircase in pictures of the *Titanic* led upstairs to more offices, more bulky desks, more shifting paper. Farther on high, in little chambers on the third floor, a priest or two was billeted. Coffee was left to stew in a staff lunchroom somewhere off the main entrance. The Archdiocese had been installed in the building a long time, and the dry must of the place was probably the molder of Church documents. For all its grandeur the atmosphere of the house was forlorn. In fact, the words *house,* not to mention *home,* seemed strange and distant terms to describe this bad dream of a dwelling.

The dark green baizelike wall coverings of the ceremonial entrance hall were mounted with massive Piranesi architectural engravings, big pearly studies of perspective. They may have been the only leftovers in the house from the Empire Builder's collection. One of the much-remarked features of the house was its art gallery, complete with a skylight and pipe organ. The relation of the pipe organ to the gallery was never clear. But everyone in the Archdiocesan office seemed to take pride in the presence of the gallery (the paintings were gone) when I went there one day as a girl, sent by the cloistered nuns of my high school to deliver a package, and was allowed to look around the place.

The Empire Builder had been a collector. He had some European masters—including a Delacroix—and more contemporary works as well. He favored monumental landscapes of the West, hoisting on the walls of his gallery and his downtown office the very lands he had girdled with his railroad. He oversaw every detail of construction for his Summit Avenue house. He even sent back for revision Louis Comfort Tiffany's first designs for the stained glass windows; the elder Hill was a man uncowed by art and attitude, confident of his taste.

His son's mansion next door was only apparently more modest, perhaps because it was light to the Empire Builder's dark; champagne to his claret. It looked like a place where you'd have fun being rich. This building, too, had passed into the hands of religion. An order of nuns owned it or perhaps simply maintained it. They used it as a retreat house for women.

Here, to Louis Hill's dreamy house, in the spring of our senior year in high school, our graduating class was sent for a weekend retreat. Thirty-two of us—and room for everyone. The nuns who ran the place were real nuns (we kept assuring ourselves) but they didn't wear habits. They had *hair.* This was very strange in 1964. The Mother Superior, an elegant woman who wore a timeless tweed suit and pumps, a strand of pearls at the neck, had a sitting room walled with books that she allowed me to visit. "You write?" she said. She, too, wrote, she confessed. Poetry.

The retreat, from Friday afternoon until after Mass on Sunday morning, was supposed to be conducted in silence. At night there was much padding around from room to room, of course, sharing Hershey bars and clasping pillows to our faces to stifle shrieks of laughter. It was a glorified sleepover.

But the silence was there, wafting over us, hours at a time in the beautiful pastel house. There was something thrilling about not being allowed to talk, walking down the generous white curving staircase from the bedrooms to the breakfast room, feeling like the chatelaine of the place. In between the retreat "conferences," inspirational talks given by a retreat director alleged by the nuns to have rapport with young people, we were encouraged to find a quiet place to sit—to read or pray or think. Given these three choices, I naturally chose to read. No one seems to have thought *Jane Eyre* strange retreat reading. In my romantic Catholic upbringing the line between literature and religion was always airily imprecise.

I planned to make my private place the little dark library that the pearl-wearing Mother Superior had opened with a key, telling me I could use it, apparently offering choice real estate to a sister poet. But on Saturday morning I came downstairs early and made a wrong turn (a house big enough to get lost in!). I found myself in a rounded room, circled with curved windows. This was the sunroom visible from my father's greenhouse. The big glassy room, round as a bowl, took in east and south. The light streamed softly in. The room seemed cantilevered over the bluff above the West Seventh flats where I had been born. On the tile floor upholstered chairs had been arranged, along with a fainting couch covered in old chintz, masses of unnecessary pillows upon it. A low table with a vase of flowers was placed by the curved windows. It was the room of my dreams, a transparent bowl to hold me like a contented fish in the curved aquarium of its glass. A room meant for reading, the light gently impressing itself, the deep quiet of a great house full of ease and daydream.

The Mother Superior had said the night before that this had been the home of an "artistic family." "I think you can see that," she said, looking around the moss-colored room where she kept her books. Or were they the books of the artistic family? I wasn't sure.

She asked if I wanted to be a writer. Oh, I did.

Well, that was good because I had come to the house of an artist. In fact, a Renaissance man—he composed music, wrote poetry, he painted pictures. And (she saved this for last) he had won an Academy Award. The movies. She paused to allow this glamour to shiver through me.

He had grown up in this house, she said. The grandson of James J. Hill. But of course he no longer lived here—I think we both understood that such a person, a painter, a composer, the winner of an Academy Award, could not live in St. Paul. He had to be elsewhere. New York, Hollywood. No, she said, he lived in the south of France.

Ah, better than Hollywood. More literary, more artistic, a place even more hallowed than the Holy City of

New York, shrine of all my usual future imaginings, bred of dust jacket author photos: *She lives in New York. . . . He divides his time between New York and Cape Cod. . . .*

"The south of France" was not simply a location as New York finally was. The south of France was a *condition*, the unreal estate of romantic ex-pat dreams. It was an indistinct yet brilliant region, a narrow band of possibility laid out like a gold filament, a precious necklace cast on the smooth flesh of beaches ancient even to the Romans, its dreamy coast punctuated by the habitations of my future arty saints whose lives and desires I already intuited— Matisse and Fitzgerald, and the girl writer I came to adore, Katherine Mansfield, she of the cool prose style and early death.

And now, it turned out, this glamorous region was home, as well, to Jerome Hill, a homeboy like Fitzgerald. I collected such local models of artistic escape. And though Hill was a lesser light in the pantheon, still he intrigued me, maybe because he seemed to have picked up the gauntlet Fitzgerald threw down, the bitter grudge against the leisure class. For Jerome Hill was crazy rich, rich the way Fitzgerald liked his heroes to be, a man who could really be imagined to possess a diamond as big as the Ritz. Instead, he had trotted off to the south of France and become an artist, and somehow got himself an Academy Award. Wealth *and* achievement. Fitzgerald had not, perhaps, counted on that combination.

Alone in the Louis Hill sunroom in the early morning, basking in silence, I opened my novel, and read about the fierce English orphan girl as I sat in the house of the son of the artistic family. I sank into the big flowers of the chintz-covered fainting couch and read about poverty, but inwardly I glittered (a Fitzgerald word) with grandeur. Because I understood long before the novel had it worked out, that Jane Eyre would not be a penniless spinster, would not teach forever in a threadbare gown in a miserable charity school. I knew she would, somehow, ascend.

But I also knew dimly, sometimes with a sharp sting, that I didn't belong in the splendor I was borrowing in this lovely room, this gigantic house. I didn't even belong in my fancy girls-school where the nuns taught us how to use fish forks. It was a fluke, bred of my parents' furious belief in education and a great aunt's influence with the nuns that I was enrolled with the daughters of the city's Catholic rich to begin with. Fitzgerald (whose mother had attended the same school in her day) knew this sensation and the odd, viral touchiness with which it attacks the soul. Fitzgerald admitted he "would always cherish an abiding distrust, an animosity, toward the leisure class— not the conviction of a revolutionist but the smoldering hatred of a peasant." The romantic "winter dreams" of Fitzgerald's ruinously ambitious working-class hero Dexter Green to possess beauty and ease in the person of the careless Judy Jones were doomed even as his outward success displaced them and he became rich and successful.

But what of the winter dreams of the rich, those who supposedly already have it all? The hardscrabble surface of raw ambition is the poor man's gold, a creative freehold. Creativity and a thirst for fame can make a king out of a poor boy. But how does the rich man pass through the eye of the needle, how does he feel the protean surge, working as Matisse did from youth—"like a drunken brute trying to kick the door down"—if all the doors are already wide open. Is he destined only to collect, never to create?

What great fortune, instead, living off the reservoir of Depression era pride as my florist father did, happily attesting to that golden age when, as he put it, *nobody had anything, not anything.* He always said this as if it were evidence of his greatest, most enduring wealth. My inheritance.

JEROME HILL, grandson of the Empire Builder, second son of Louis Hill (also a railroad man, patron of the arts, passionate amateur photographer), was born in this lovely house in 1905, nearly nine years after Scott Fitzgerald was born in a lesser house on a lesser street in the same neighborhood. Jerome Hill graduated from Yale with a music major, and from the late twenties made his main residence in Cassis, a fishing village along the same stretch of the Mediterranean as Matisse's wild beast territory in Collioure. Cassis was also the summer home for migrating members of the Bloomsbury set, especially the painters. Vanessa Bell leased a house and painting studio there between the two wars, and Virginia and Leonard Woolf, after staying in a hotel in town, almost leased a property as well before thinking better of such a commitment. Katherine

Mansfield, too, had come to Cassis, in one of her first of many attempts to find a home in the sun along the Mediterranean coast.

Were it not for the Academy Award for best documentary film (for a documentary portrait of Albert Schweitzer), Hill might be dismissed as a gifted dilettante. That would be a mistake. Jerome Hill wasn't exactly a dilettante. He was that rare bird—a free artist. Free because of wealth, because of temperament, circumstance, the mixed bag of nature and nurture it is impossible to prize apart into an explanation of personality and accomplishment. Another St. Paul escapee, gone across the sea to find not only the sun but the life of art.

Recognized as an artist from childhood, encouraged and directed in his talent from his earliest years by his "artistic family," Hill's painting does suggest the amiability of an ardent student. The canvases, bedazzled with sparkling color, the fizzle of sea air about them, mark him as a diligent retracer of the light-obsessed generations of French painters dating from the Impressionists. They especially connect him to Matisse who gathered with his friends—Derain, Vlaminck—on the bright coast of the

Mediterranean to paint their wild-beast paintings during the very year of Jerome Hill's birth in frozen Minnesota.

Hill's real kinship, which shows up in his films, was not to any art form but to the avant-garde, that corner of modern art that resolutely retains the rights of the sandbox, of childhood games and handmade objects. The word *experimental* is usually associated with avant-garde artists as if they constituted art's pure science, the lab for the rest of creative endeavor, a way station for future advances in form, or investigations in the opposite direction, as if digging for buried shards like archaeologists. But there is another way of looking at the place of the avant-garde: its artists can refuse to serve either the future or the traditions of the past, but pledge themselves radically to elemental gestures of human expression—Yoko Ono's primal screams, the silences of John Cage.

Jerome Hill, so apparently obedient to the best efforts and projects of the past in his painting, found in movie work a canvas free of the past's instructions and greatness. Hill steered clear of Hollywood, drawn to documentary not because he favored nonfiction but because it allowed him freedom from the studios, the unions, the whole professional moviemaking apparatus. The rich man would enter the kingdom of film by choosing the poor man's form—practically the humility of the home movie. He refused, apparently instinctively, to work on feature films, the great collaborative form of the twentieth century—collaborative in part because it is the most expensive art form in the history of human expression, at least as it is practiced in America. Jerome Hill held, instead, to the chamber work of independent filmmaking, to portraiture, and finally, in his last and best attempt, to autobiography, that most home-brewed of genres.

"The me that am . . . but never will be again. Hold on to a single moment, even for a second, and it already belongs to the past." With this prosaic observation, spoken in an attractively laconic voice, Jerome Hill begins his narration of his autobiographical film, *Film Portrait.* The voice-over accompanies a sequence of Hill shaving. The ordinariness of this routine activity and the unremarkable, if philosophical, voice-over perfectly represent his style: casual, benignly wry, cheerfully aristocratic, and modest. This is a man who can spend many frames on close-ups of his own face and convey not intimacy but an almost scientific, or at least objective, detachment.

At the time, Jerome Hill was in his midsixties, and although *Film Portrait* was to be his last film, apparently he didn't yet know about the cancer that would end his life late in 1971. The film won the 1972 London Film Festival award for best documentary.

Jerome Hill belonged to the first generation of movie-goers, and the prevailing theme of *Film Portrait* (and the point of its title) is that he and the movies were born at the same moment and, in his view, grew up together. For him, movies were forever new, young, experimental. It was in their nature to be provisional and independent, a matter of one person with a magic box catching light, seeing the world afresh. They were not a "production."

Jerome Hill is still referred to by those who knew him as a Renaissance man, just as the Mother Superior of my senior retreat invoked him as we sat in what I now realize, from scenes in *Film Portrait,* must have been his mother's sitting room. He had many gifts, "almost too many," his friend Otto Lang says in *The Man in the Portrait,* a film eulogy for Hill made shortly after his death. With his degree in music composition from Yale, he wrote music throughout his life, including the score for *Film Portrait*—impressionistic, French in the manner of Satie and "Les Six" composers like Poulenc. Though he was best known professionally as a filmmaker, he thought of himself, perhaps primarily, as an artist and devoted himself steadfastly to painting. He also wrote poetry. And he gave away money.

He had a lot of it to give. His childhood was positively Nabokovian in its splendor, with a background not simply of wealth, but of taste, art, thoughtful travel, and long dreamy days. Besides a lively family life in the elegant Summit Avenue house, there were trips to France (he was not simply bilingual, but bicultural practically from birth, the son of a Francophile mother), long train rides west into Indian country, summers riding horses at North Oaks, the immense family farm north of St. Paul.

It was a privileged, liberal American childhood with a late–Russian Empire tang. It seems to have been a life destined by birth and sensibility for art. "Good," the Empire Builder is reported to have said, observing his three little grandsons, "one for the railroad, one for the bank, one for the arts," as if the whole of life arranged itself tidily into just these categories.

When Jerome Hill turns to "the me that was" in *Film Portrait,* he turns not to himself but, as if instinctively, to time itself. "1905," he says in his dry, faintly amused voice. "More curious than glorious, the year of my birth." The crammed interiors of the age appear festooned with aspidistras and antimacassars. In an invitation to shared judgment, he remarks, "Was there ever a period more ugly?" A nonchalant comment, but it establishes an authority for his voice, and therefore for his story: a man of unquestioned aesthetic judgment is running this life, this movie. "Thank God for Louis Tiffany," he says, and the camera surveys a series of Tiffany glass lamp shades and windows glowing and manipulated by the painterly hand of Hill's editing.

He plays the high card of his family wealth and prominence early, with characteristic ease. "My grandfather," he acknowledges as a portrait of the steely old man appears. And then adds casually, "He was in the railroad business." Hill isn't coy, any more than he is confessional. He mentions the family's Scotch-Irish immigration to Canada, and then, in a single sentence, places his family in a world that explains his background: "They had, in one immense leap, become important people." Not rich, not successful—important.

I relished that line when I first saw *Film Portrait* in my twenties, about the same time I saw Matisse's *Woman Before an Aquarium*. It was a movie so different from my notion of what a movie was—and showing pictures of St. Paul—that I was captivated. *Film Portrait* conveyed a familiarity that had nothing to do with personal revelation, but relied on the unexpected intimacy of the narrator's voice. I hardly understood that this was "an experimental film."

This was simply the first time a movie had ever come to me like a personal letter, as direct and unmediated an utterance as poetry, one human being to another—or to himself—musing. I did not expect movies to speak directly to me or to speak somehow to themselves as books did, as poems did. Movies were immense seductions, grand and imposing *productions*—the word was a movie word, and apt. Didn't everyone love the movies? But they were not the human voice, alone and free, telling its bit of life news to a single listener in the way that a book did. There was something large and communal about movies. It was right that they were on "the big screen": they were writ too large for anything but a wall.

But here was a movie that belonged to a modest, intimate world. A poor man's movie. It did not speak solely through pictures and dialogue like feature films (which, to me, were "real movies"). Nor was this man speaking in the godly style of documentary as "a narrator," nor in the anonymous information-giving voice-overs of certain old-fashioned feature films, usually adaptations from classic novels.

Besides, I knew Jerome Hill spoke the truth: in St. Paul, the Hills *were* important. Indeed, they were important beyond St. Paul, but somehow it was a St. Paul way of looking at things, of saying things. On the one hand eliding any crude reference to money, on the other inflating the condition of wealth with magnificence, moving a half step toward divinity. A very F. Scott Fitzgerald way of seeing things—which is itself a very St. Paul way of seeing things. Hill's was a real voice, speaking from a life, not a narration.

And I was listening to a memoir, the genre that inhabits a fascinatingly indeterminate narrative space between fiction and documentary. As it refines its point of view, lavishing itself on the curious habits of personal consciousness, memoir achieves a rare detachment even as it enters more deeply into the revelation of individual consciousness. Its greatest intimacy (the display of perception) paradoxically reveals its essential impersonality. It wishes to see the world, not itself. Hill's real subject, like Matisse's, was individual perception: not simply *what* was seen, but *how* seeing was experienced. How it "conveyed all one's emotions," as Matisse put it.

It didn't concern me that Jerome Hill wasn't telling his secrets, that I wasn't getting the scoop. Some years after I first saw *Film Portrait,* when I learned that Hill was gay, I wondered whether he had felt constrained from allowing that fact to surface in the film, whether he had wanted to speak of it. But he seemed so intent on his lifelong love affair with film as the story he was telling in the film that I didn't feel cheated that he had suppressed or avoided the subject. (Though the case for conscious suppression is right in the film: in his visual list of possible selves, he displays a photo of himself with Brigitte Bardot, very *intime* on the Côte d'Azur where he had his main residence in

Cassis. Without other information, the photo steers the viewer naturally to assume this is one possible scenario he would relish living more fully.) Who can say? Hill made his movie in 1971, a time already very distant.

Like all true memoirists, Hill is drawn more to shards than to stories, images rather than narrative. He notes his recollection of first sounds (chimes of a clock: "the fact that it told time only interested me much later"), early sensations of light. His first "moving picture," re-created in *Film Portrait,* is a series of drawings on the corners of pages of the dictionary that could be flipped to show the *Titanic* going down. An innate fascination with illusion, magic tricks, and mystery pervades all his games. "Where," he asks, "do children's games lead?"

The question draws him to an early memory of napping on a chaise longue in his mother's room, the very room, I felt certain, where I had sat with the poetry-writing Mother Superior with the good pearls. Hill's memory is presented in *Film Portrait* in a sequence of water-colors he painted directly on the negatives, as if he couldn't keep his hands off the film. In these drawings, a boy is put to bed near a window by a woman in a long Edwardian gown. The figures are manipulated slowly, like stately paper dolls: the child lies in bed and the woman tenderly (if rather stiffly, given the purposely crude animation) draws a coverlet up to his chin.

The paper-doll mother pulls down the window's dark outer shade and then an inner white shade. Outside, the sound of horses' hooves can be heard—the sounds of a dying era, pre-movie-era sounds. (Hill paints bright jumping animated cars in front of the photograph of the mansion with its horse-drawn carriage pulled up to the porte cochere.) The boy is drawn to a hole ("like an eye") in the shade. Pulling the inner shade closer, away from the darker outer shade, the child discovers the principle of camera obscura, his Empire Builder grandfather's castle appearing suddenly tiny and complete, upside down on the "screen" of the shade. A profound intimacy radiates from this sequence. Children's games lead, it seems, directly to the adult imagination and in a Möbius strip of relation loops back to the family from which he has sprung.

In a fortunate coincidence of wealth and hobby, Hill's father was a camera buff. Very early he became a movie buff, too. Films were brought to the house for private showings—to avoid the "microbes" of the public movie house. The reels of these early emulsion films could not be rented; they had to be bought. "What a privilege," Hill says, "to learn pieces of film by heart, as if they were music." The humble reverence of his voice is a reminder of how far in the cultural past 1971 is: his is the world before Blockbuster Video, before the VCR and DVD player.

Hill includes in *Film Portrait* some very early clips by Georges Méliès and other early filmmakers. He includes, as well, snippets of professional-quality home movies, shot by a Pathé cameraman who "frequently came to film us kids." And there they are, young people on horses at the North Oaks Farm, the Pathé cameraman displaying his revolutionary technique, the traveling shot. It was an advance in filmmaking that appeared in the Hill home movies before most people saw it in feature films in a movie house.

This display of family moments has a homely charm, everyone mugging for the camera, tumbling around in a Buster Keatonish way. And then, disrupting the high jinks, the voice again: "These people to whom I belonged curiously did not belong to me," Hill says—as usual with an easy neutrality. "Of everything they did so well, I was incapable." It is not clear what they did "so well"—ride horses? Anyway, he goes on to make his point: "I was living a life apart." It is one of the film's rare personal revelations.

The film's only extended narrative sequence concerns a trip the Hill family took across his grandfather's rails into Indian country. The trip was a diplomatic mission of sorts to the Blackfoot Indians, to gain access across their lands. The voice remains detached, capable of remorseless statement: The railroad—his family—had "no scruples about moving in and disrupting the lives of these people," he says. The voice is degrees cooler than the rest of his urbane narration.

As for himself, a boy of twelve, he absorbed "the beauty of this aboriginal world." He learned the complicated Blackfoot sign language and played games with the children. At the end of the summer he was accepted into the tribe by an ancient blind woman. "I had become a Blackfoot," he says. "At last I had a name I didn't share with anyone else. Here ends my childhood."

And here ends the self-as-camera part of the film, the deep immersion in the mysterious sources of perception that belong to childhood. He leaps over key developmental teenage years without incident or remark, arriving at adulthood from childhood as if by parachute. From then on, the memoir belongs to the movie camera and follows more closely his observation and involvement in *its* technical coming-of-age. For by the time he is twenty-three, he, the conscious artist — not his hobbyist father and not the hired Pathé cameramen — holds the movie camera.

In his film autobiography Jerome Hill uses his seaside villa at Cassis and his early experimental films from the thirties (if some of his sillier stuff — a whole short film, for example, with everybody doing everything backward — can be weighed down by the term "experimental") to return to the idea of the birth of film as an art. As it happens (or maybe it is no coincidence, but a fact integral to Hill's attachment to Cassis), the very first strip of film ever shown to a paying public (in 1895) was of a train arriving at the La Ciotat platform, the nearest station to Cassis, a film shot by the Lumière brothers.

That first film clip shows a roaring train engine — the perfect image to speak to the grandson of the Empire Builder. The train approaches the antique figures on the platform, coming right at us in the audience. It must have been an electrifying experience to sit in the black box of a hired hall in 1895 and see that engine charging at you. Hill tucks this historic Lumière train clip into *Film Portrait* more than once. Then he ends his autobiography with his own contemporary homage shot of the same scene, in color, a sleek new train rolling in on the same platform, at the same angle, though the woman waiting at the side wears a short skirt and does not hold a parasol.

Why, I wondered, as I sat watching the movie again recently at a library archive in St. Paul, is this man so moving to me—a man who does not display himself, who prefers the gracious surface to the frank revelation, a man—all right—who is finally if not a dilettante, an amateur. A man hidden behind the scrim of his easeful life and obscured identity. Is it *because* of his essential shyness in the face of the personal genre he has chosen? Because he *can't* tell all or even indicate much about himself? And does this reticence convey a greater, more enduring human truth than disclosure ever can?

Beyond the joy and glory of color that he shared with Matisse, who also had gravitated to the blue coast, Jerome

Hill perhaps shared as well Matisse's belief in "the deep gravity that persists in every human being": The acknowledgment of privacy, of the unknowable world that beats like a pulse behind the blue fretwork screen that Matisse lugged back from Morocco and used in so many of his harem paintings and in the painting in the Chicago Art Institute that first captivated me. Jerome Hill remains elusive, even as he presents his life in the fragmentary images of his movie memoir.

Every person's life, we say, is a story. In fact, when a life becomes story, a person knows he has "a life." The narrative instinct sorts, orders, represses, highlights, finessing its way to a certain contour—not to "reality," and certainly not to "the truth," but to shapeliness. To represent the whole of reality is beyond the capacity of art, even outside its desire. In fact, the inability to limit the flow of reality into the mind is one definition of madness.

Once entered, the house of memory claims power even over the alchemist, that identity Hill chose for himself in the final frames of his movie. In the end, the magic man with all the tricks up his sleeve is no match for time's imperial transformations and memory's botched bookkeeping.

In *Film Portrait* Jerome Hill holds up the brightly colored bits of his life and work to the southern sun, along that paradisal strip of seaside France that lured so many others before and after him. There, from the darkened room of the camera, he stalked the light of the past that he must have believed held the truth of himself, though he knew that truth to be inexpressible, lost after all in the northern shadows his family had claimed and that he had fled.

FIVE

Les Bains Turcs

*I*n 1683 the Turkish army of Mustafa the Black (also the Terrible—the Europeans piled on the scary adjectives) surged west, threatening the easternmost imperial capital of Christendom on September 12 at the Battle of Vienna. The successful European repulsion of the invaders is directly credited to Georg Franz Kolschitzky, a Turkish-speaking Pole (or Armenian—the sources vary) working for a trader in oriental wares, who made his way through enemy lines to give Charles of Lorraine (or King Sobiesky—more scholarly dispute) the intelligence he needed to outwit the rampaging armies of the Ottoman Empire.

In their flight, the retreating Turks left behind five hundred sacks of "dry black fodder"—coffee. With the award (or theft?) of this war bounty, Kolschitzky opened Vienna's first coffeehouse, Zur Blauen Flasche, the Blue Bottle.

So goes the tale, the moral being that the Turks, by means of this dark elixir, conquered the Europeans after all, initiating the Continent into the comforts of the coffeehouse and layabout society. A stealth victory for the oriental pleasure culture and its ideology of leisure.

Beyond coffee drinking, the epitome of the pleasure culture, East or West, is embodied in the time-wasting luxury of the bath. The Romans had considered the baths essential to their *otium cum dignitate,* the dignified leisure, the absence from business activity, at the root of their conception of a civilized society. The Central European lands of early modern times carried forward this theme with their own medicinal variation—the spa. The most renowned spa, Karlovy Vary (Carlsbad) in Bohemia, was founded in 1350 near warm mineral springs by Charles IV, the Holy Roman Emperor. During the eighteenth century it became the spa of choice for the European elite, most famously Goethe and Peter the Great. J. S. Bach took the waters there, as did Casanova and Schiller, Gogol and Liszt.

But the European spa was not *le bain turc.* It was hygienic and improving, a genteel retreat of several weeks combining a course of treatment with edifying cultural events (concerts, lectures), everyone dressed to the nines. It was not an Ingres painting, not a vision of soporific pleasure. In fact, the spa culture catered to dispirit and the narcissism of self-improvement. It was useful to possess a *complaint*—a poor liver was ideal—to indulge in this AWOL behavior.

What *le bain turc* and the spa had in common was not sensuality (the East) or hygiene (the West), but a dream of ease, a brush with the Golden Age: days passed amid the leisurely contemplation of passing details, drawing a lazy finger across the surface of scented water in a warm pool of peachy marble, reaching for a sugared date, gazing at white birds warbling in a silver cage, watching, like the thoughtful subject of *Woman Before an Aquarium* in Chicago, fish glinting in a bowl. In fact, the idea was to become something of a fish oneself, floating in a watery social medium, free of the usual associations, the routine social circle.

But the Turkish bath embodied the Golden Age ideal with a splendor and indulgence that the uptight grandeur of the Central European spas could not allow themselves to imagine. And the baths represented a golden age of female society, the sweets and gossip of sorority girls lolling about, dishing about lipstick and boys.

No wonder that arch journal-keeper Anaïs Nin, ardent would-be sensualist and self-imaginer, made her way to Morocco in the thirties and "fell in love with Fez," taking tea with rock sugar and accepting from her hosts little almond cakes covered with a silk handkerchief set on a copper tray, noting as she walked in the market streets "an Arab asleep over his bag of saffron, another praying with his beads while selling herbs." She had found, she thought, a world of perfect indulgence and unbroken leisure.

She was invited here, invited there, visiting the lovely shadowy homes of elegant people for whom "it is a mortal insult . . . to seem hurried." The whole nature of relations between people "does not depend so much on conversation or exchange as in the creation of a propitious, dreamy, meditative, contemplative atmosphere, a mood." She was invited to a harem. "Seven wives of various ages but all of them fat," she records, "sat around a low table eating candy and dates. We discussed nail polish." Intelligence Delacroix and Matisse could not have been expected to tease out of the corners of the harem.

Eventually, Nin followed a group of women to the baths. She went by way of "complex streets. Anonymous walls. Secret luxury." Before she even got there she was living in fiction, the dream of her imagining. She joined the women in disrobing without a murmur. They, however, took forever to emerge from their many skirts and several blouses "which looked like bandages . . . so much white muslin linen, cotton to unroll, unfold and fold again on the bench."

In the steam room, all the women sat on the floor, filling pails of water from fountains, pouring the water over their heads, soaping themselves, steam filling the room. Nin, tiny as a dancer and proud of it, was agog at the sheer bulk of these women. "All of them were enormous," she writes. "The flesh billowed, curved, folded in tremendous heavy waves. They seemed to be sitting on pillows of flesh of all colors from the pale Northern Arab skin to the African." As the water they sat in darkened with filth and the debris from the depilatories they used, she could not bring herself to wash her face with the soap they handed her, which had scrubbed their feet, their armpits.

She wanted "to see the Arab women clothed again, concealed in yards of white cotton." She wanted to see their faces but not their bodies: "Such beautiful heads had risen out of these mountains of flesh, heads of incredible perfection, dazzling eyes, heavily fringed, sensual features. . . . But these heads rose from formless masses of flesh, heaving like plants in the sea, swelling, swaying, falling, the breasts like sea anemones, floating, the stomachs of perpetually pregnant women, the legs like pillows, the backs like cushions, the hips with furrows like a mattress."

The Moroccan women were equally dismayed by her meager body: "They asked was I adolescent. I had no fat on me. I must be a girl." In this assessment another misapprehension emerges, this time on the part of the East looking at the West: The thin, slight woman must be a girl. She is the adolescent goddess, the eternal ingenue. The fountain of youth turns out not to be a gushing elixir but its opposite—the willingness to take in nothing, to starve and eliminate, to attenuate. No Turkish delight on this menu.

Extreme thinness—anorexia and its various cousins—possesses a purely lyric power, flexing the paradoxical might of innocence ("I had no fat on me. I must be a girl"). Because what is weak (what is thin) can do no wrong, can enforce no demand, it must be blameless. It can be a victim (more weakness), but it cannot be a perpetrator (no strength). With only a negligible body, it remains pure spirit. Being spirit, it can believe itself harmless—as flesh and body can never claim to be. It is a virgin. Because these sylphs tend to be women, the identity they project is that of the ingenue. Inviolate—but intriguing, tantalizing.

As Thackeray remarks about his wild-thing heroine in *Vanity Fair,* "When attacked sometimes, Becky had a knack of adopting a demure *ingénue* air, under which she was most dangerous." Fat is frank. It has indulged itself. It cannot deny the body and its sins. And what is more treacherous than a person, lean and hungry, who believes herself to be without fault, without the capacity to wound?

The journal-writing voyeur, vain of her wand-thin body and her soulfulness, gazes at the goddesses of leisure, of indulgence. And reports on the shameful fat of living, the dirt, the debris.

DELACROIX HAD EXPERIENCED an "exaltation" that even "sherbets and fruits could barely appease" in 1832 when he was allowed to pass through a door, along "a dark corridor" to sketch, in the spirit of stealth, a harem in Algiers. Flaubert, on the other hand, traveled to Egypt with his randy pal Maxime Du Camp in 1849 on a trip that combined mosque sightings with sex tourism. They managed to gain access to exoticism mainly by frequenting Cairo prostitutes. "Tomorrow we are to have a party on the river," he wrote to a friend at home, "with several whores dancing to the sound of *darabukehs* and castanets, their hair spangled with gold piastres."

This tendency toward the exotic was even stronger, it seemed, than his lust: "Oh, how willingly I would give up all the women in the world to possess the mummy of Cleopatra," he had written as a Byron-besotted youth, burning for the shimmering East.

During his 1849 trip, on December 1, a Saturday night at ten o'clock (he meticulously notes all this), Flaubert writes to his best friend Louis Bouilhet of his sexual high jinks in Cairo. He and Du Camp (later a writer of travel books) had gone to a brothel, a place "dilapidated and open to all the winds and lit by a night-light." They could see a palm tree through the windowless window. The Turkish women wore silk robes embroidered with gold. The usual set design, the requisite exotic costumes. It was, he wrote, "a great place for contrasts: splendid things gleam in the dust."

Then the report: "I performed on a mat that a family of cats had to be shooed off—a strange coitus, looking at each other without being able to exchange a word, and the exchange of looks is all the deeper for the curiosity and the surprise. My brain was too stimulated for me to enjoy it much otherwise. These shaved cunts make a strange effect—the flesh is hard as bronze."

Next morning, December 2, it's time to write Maman: "Here we are in Cairo, my darling, where we shall probably stay the entire month of December, until the return of the pilgrims from Mecca." And so on and so forth, finally offering an Eagle Scout's inventory of "what I wear these days . . . flannel body-belt, flannel shirt, flannel drawers, thick trousers, warm vest, thick neck-cloth, with an overcoat besides morning and evening."

A day later, in his private travel notes, the cool sex tourist and the good mama's boy disappear. The eye steadies, the voice speaks modestly from the echoing chamber of pure description: "The Nile is dotted with white sails; the two large sails, crossed like a *fichu,* make the boat look like a flying swallow with two immense wings. The sky is completely blue, hawks wheel about us; below, far down, men are small, moving noiselessly. The liquid light seems to penetrate the surface of things and enter into them."

He has ceased to be a braggart and a smooth talker. He says only what he sees: he has become a painter, washed clean of attitude, of pose, taking his notes, making a pure sketch.

FOR ALL THE FEVERED efforts of traveling artists and writers, the only people who could hope to gain extended access to the forbidden domain of the harem, that tabernacle of perfume and spice, were women. For an eyewitness account of harem life, generations of male English and French travelers or would-be travelers in the eighteenth and nineteenth centuries relied principally on Lady Mary Wortley Montagu's dispatches from a journey through the Ottoman Empire, which she undertook when her husband was sent as ambassador to Constantinople. They arrived in 1717 for what was supposed to be a lengthy posting to the Sublime Porte.

Wortley proved to be a dismal failure as a diplomat and was recalled after fifteen months. But it was time enough for Lady Mary to take her notes. Her *Embassy Letters* were published in 1763, the year after her death, though they were known to a select circle during her lifetime, as Anaïs

Nin's diary was famous long before its sensational publishing success in the 1970s.

The recipients of Lady Mary's *Letters* included some of the literary lights of the age, including Alexander Pope who, as a hunchback, betrayed the touching hope to Lady Mary that the taste for the exotic in the Orient might confirm the rumor that cultivated women of the Levant "best like the Ugliest fellows, as the most admirable productions of nature, and look upon Deformities as the Signatures of divine Favour."

A century after Lady Mary's travels, stay-at-home exoticist Ingres counted on a brief passage about her visit to a bathhouse to provide the imagery for his famous *Le Bain Turc*. "There were 200 women," Lady Mary wrote of her visit to the bath. "The sofas were covered with cushions and rich carpets, on which sat the ladies, all being in a state of nudity . . . yet there was not a wanton smile or immodest gesture among them." The essential elements of the pleasure culture were there—evident leisure, ample flesh, lavish stage set. Ingres faithfully painted the words.

For all her delight in gleefully dressing up in Turkish costume, enjoying the anonymity and privacy of a veiled

face (and perhaps glad of the chance to cover her disfigur-
ing smallpox scars), Lady Mary's view of the harem was
exactly the opposite of those of the men who either never
saw it (Ingres); who beheld it only briefly—perhaps as a
tableau expressly arranged to meet a Western visitor's ex-
pectations (Delacroix); or whose exotic couplings were
purchased retail (Flaubert).

Not only was there no "wanton smile or immodest gesture" in the massed odalisques Lady Mary observed at the
bath, the harem bondage motif was absent as well. There
was a tendency for Western male visitors, artists and writers both, to conflate the bath and the harem, the nudity
presumed in the bath slopping over, so to speak, into the
luxurious living quarters where the women are shown or
described as supine and nude or semiclothed upon divans,
as if reclining in a warm tub.

Alexander Pope had teased Lady Mary before her de-
parture, saying he expected her to abandon herself "to extreme Effeminancy, Laziness, and Lewdness of Life."
"Laziness" being the dirty word for *leisure* and "Lewdness"
being the natural twin of either. Turkey, he reminded her
with a wink, was known as "the Land of Jealousy, where

the unhappy Women converse with none but Eunuchs, and where the very Cucumbers are brought to them Cutt." A man's world, in other words, the women displayed like chocolates in a satin box.

That's not what Lady Mary found. When she arrived dressed in her traveling costume at the *hammam,* the elite public bath, she was finally persuaded by the gracious entreaties of "the lady that seemed the most considerable among them" to disrobe and join the relaxed atmosphere of the bath. She at last opened her blouse and the women saw with dismay her corset. They now understood her hesitation to disrobe and met it with grave compassion: "they believed I was so locked up in that machine, that it was not in my own power to open it, which contrivance they attributed to my husband."

The reclining odalisque had finally caught a glimpse of the vertical European lady. And what the relaxed Turkish harem dweller saw as she gazed at the corseted European was what the Western observer saw looking at the harem: a bird in a cage, a fish in a bowl. Prisoners "tied up . . . in little boxes of the shape of their bodies" as Lady Mary's Turkish hostess exclaimed, horrified by the corset, which finally revealed the secret of the Western woman's ram-rod carriage.

From this moment at the bath Lady Mary, according to her biographer Robert Halsband, "began to develop the paradox of Turkish women's liberty and English women's slavery." She loved to go out veiled, free to move about, observing the marketplace and the town from beneath the little roofed room of her silk garments. This, paradoxically, was liberty.

The cloister of the harem, as far as Lady Mary could tell, was a free space for women, a private environment ruled by women's taste, devoted to women's ways, where no husband or father or brother could interfere. When Lady Mary dined with the Sultana in 1718 she was served "a dinner of fifty dishes of meat" amid magnificence. "The knives were of gold, the hafts set with diamonds but the piece of luxury that gripped my eyes was the tablecloth and napkins, which were all tiffany, embroidered with silks and gold, in the finest manner, in natural flowers."

The Sultana herself was dressed in dazzling garments, weighted with jewels of which "no European queen has half the quantity." The room where Lady Mary was led was large, "with a sofa the whole length of it, adorned with white pillars . . . covered with pale-blue figured velvet on a silver ground, with cushions of the same, where I was desired to repose till the Sultana appeared."

Lady Mary came to admire Islam as well. After a long theological talk with Achmet Bey, a learned effendi who was her tutor in the ways of his country, she was delighted to reassure her correspondents at home that enlightened Turks, like educated Christians, "put superstition and revelation into their theology only to win the credence of the ignorant; and the Alcoran [Koran] itself contained only the purest morality."

In fact, Lady Mary airily reported to her at-home correspondents, Islam was best understood as a kind of deism — the very way her Enlightenment soul had settled the vexing religious hash of her own Christian tradition with its embarrassing revelatory nonsense. "I explained to him the difference between the religion of England and Rome," she says briskly, "and he was pleased to hear there were Christians that did not worship images, or adore the Virgin Mary."

The wonder of Turkish life was that, on the one hand,

it was exotic and on the other . . . it wasn't. Harem life offered a woman not servitude and imprisonment, but opulence and astonishing personal freedom. Take away the jewels and the garden fountains and the diamond-encrusted knives (though she, for one, would prefer to keep them), and you still had domestic independence of a sort Lady Mary could only envy. The harem, the women's private quarters, provided not a caged life, but a silken chamber, something more akin to what Virginia Woolf two centuries later would memorably call "a room of one's own."

AND WHAT OF the word itself? *Odalisque.* The definition in the *OED,* conjuring all the sex slave imagery of the West's heated imaginings, turns out to be a fabricaton of that very imagining. The root, *oda,* is simply the Turkish word for "room"—you see it today in Anatolian towns, advertising B&Bs. It is the *chambre libre* and *zimmer frei* of low-cost tourist lodging.

Predictably, the first appearance of the word *oda* in English, in 1625, came from a "Voyage writer," as Lady Mary called them. "They have Roomes," Samuel Purchas writes in *Pilgrims II* of his observations in Turkey, "which the Turkes call Oda's, but we may more properly (in regard of the use they are put unto) call them Schooles."

Out of this chaste schoolgirl beginning emerge the sultry beauties of Western art and Western dreaming. Yet, even as late as 1822 Byron still employs the word in *Don Juan* to mean a chamber or perhaps the aggregate of its inhabitants: "Upstarted all The Oda, in a general commotion."

By 1886, deep in Victoria's reign, Richard Burton in his *Arabian Nights* (the *OED*'s final citation for *oda*) has nudged the word's meaning firmly from the chamber to its occupants, though like Lady Mary's bathing companions they lack wanton smiles and immodest gestures: "The women made ready the sweetmeats . . . and distributed them among all the Odahs of the Harem."

As for *odalisque* itself: according to the *OED,* the word is "corrupt." Meaning (again the *OED* speaks) "destroyed in purity, debased; altered from the original or correct condition by ignorance, carelessness, additions, etc; vitiated by errors or alternations." In this case, presumably, by wanton wishing: Samuel Purchas's Turkish Schoole Roomes turn by degrees of English (and French) imaginings into bowers of sensuous bliss, furnished with silks and gleaming gold, lovely women scattered about like decorative pillows.

The first appearance in English of the word *odalisque* shows up in 1681, in Thomas Blount's *Glossographia* (itself worth noting: a dictionary interpreting the "hard words of whatsoever language, now used in our refined English tongue," compiled by an ardent Roman Catholic whose impolitic religion kept him from his profession—the law—thus causing him to retire to his Worcestershire estate where he turned to amateur lexicography in an effort to while away his own no-doubt sequestered, overleisured days). Blount dispatches the mysterious odalisque in a bold stroke: "a Slave," he says, and is done.

The next sightings, over the seventeenth and eighteenth centuries, even straying into the nineteenth, jockey back and forth between the slave definition ("A feast . . . In honor of fair Zoradone prepar'd, Where every odalisc the labour shar'd"—Sotheby's translation of Wieland's *Oberon* in 1798 where the servant girls, and *not* the love interest, are the odalisques) and the obverse, the unemployed kept-woman/concubine whose only job description is love sweet love (Byron's "lovely Odalisques" of 1823 in *Don Juan*).

The tussle between these two opposing odalisques resolves itself by 1874 when, in an atmospheric piece by A. O'Shaughnessy titled *Music and Moonlight,* the lounging woman illogically appears by being invisible: "An Odalisc, unseen, Splendidly couched on piled-up cushions green." Though "unseen," the voluptuary vanquishes the slave girl.

Jump to 1903 and Shaw, in a letter to a mature actress, counsels, "What you want is a repertory of plays which you can carry on your own shoulders, and in which you cannot come into competition with the young odalisques of the west end." Barely a dozen years later the apparently seductive illogic of the invisibility/presence of the harem girl emerges again, this time in Joyce. He remarks of a woman that "she leans back against the pillowed wall: odalisque-featured in the luxurious obscurity." In yet another odalisque oxymoron echoing O'Shaughnessy's and Joyce's confusion (though in a different way), Arnold

Bennett in *Lord Raingo* (1926) maintains that "withal she was no odalisque. She tried to improve herself, to make herself interesting to him"—as if making yourself "interesting" to a man weren't at least part of the purpose of lounging about half-naked on pillowed divans in the first place.

Finally, in the *OED*'s last sighting, in 1967, our girl, now fully modern, riles a contemporary art critic in the March 16 *Listener* who brings us back where we started—to the visual images that have, more successfully than language, defined the term: "Is the creation of a cubist odalisque 'of consequence,'" this sour voice asks, employing the imperious quotation marks of critical irritation, "and the devoutly humble production of an ikon not?"

In 1932 MATISSE is sixty-two, living in Nice. His wife, Amélie, is a fretful invalid. Even without knowing the backstory, which was quite successfully kept in the biographical shadows until Hilary Spurling's biographies in this century, the photographs of the period suggest tension: Matisse upright in his burgher's suit; Mme Matisse with her strong face, the brow set, the mouth stern. Somehow, she has the goods on him. They have lived apart and together, *en famille* and at a distance, for years maintaining the union, refusing any of the public (or perhaps private) erotic antics of Picasso. Theirs is not a bohemian life.

Mme Matisse has given long loyalty to the great man's demanding enterprise; she is a woman who was courted with the warning she chose not to heed: "Mademoiselle, I love you dearly, but I shall always love painting more." But this has been a marriage of many paintings, many models spread supine upon the studio's patterned divan. She becomes an odalisque in her own way: a mysterious invalid, unable to do much, this capable woman who kept the family bravely together with her hat shop and her faith in her man during the long lean years before there was a whiff of success. The same woman who, some few years in the future, will rise to be a heroine again, working dangerously for the Resistance, arrested and imprisoned. But now during the interwar years—taken to her bed, requiring a companion.

Into this tense matrimonial hothouse arrives Lydia Delectorskaya, still a girl, bearing her delectable name.

She is hired to help scrape paintings, set up the studio—and attend to Mme Matisse. And then, "after several months or perhaps a year, Matisse's grim and penetrating stare began focusing on me."

Lydia had come to Nice, a Russian émigré with no French, burdened with the legal problems that often beset refugees. She turned to modeling, before being hired by Matisse, because it didn't require the usual work permits and language skills.

But she had hoped never again to work as a model. The job with Matisse was an answer to her prayers. "From the time I had work as a companion on a steady basis," she writes, "I wanted to think I was forever through with modeling, which I had found detestable. . . . Besides, there was this: I was not 'his type.'" She was blonde, "very blonde," whereas with the exception of his daughter Marguerite, "most of the models who had inspired him were southern types."

But the "grim and penetrating stare" had fixed on her. Soon Mme Matisse lost her girl, and Matisse found his. Lydia stayed with him (always "Mme Delectorskaya," Matisse's manners demanding this formality) until the end of his life, always his assistant, never his wife, his companion but not a mistress in the Picasso way. There may have been passion, but a celibate rectitude seemed to reign, a labor-intensive companionship where Lydia does the heavy lifting for the old, now-weakened Matisse, and he gives her pride of place in the creative process, the abstract lovemaking of art making.

In any case, she came with nothing and years later, immediately after his death, Delectorskaya left with nothing—this was no gold digger. Upon Matisse's death, she decamped with the valise she had kept packed. But during her long tenancy, Mme Matisse was outraged by her presence and driven to extremes. Mme Matisse finally stormed away from the Nice apartment. "No one who creates," Matisse said cryptically acknowledging his wife's right to feel betrayed, "is blameless." Henri and Amélie Matisse never again met in person.

Matisse felt his models were "never just 'extras' in an interior." In fact, he said, "I depend absolutely on my model, whom I observe at liberty, and then I decide on the pose which best suits *her nature*. When I take a new model, it is from the unselfconscious attitudes she takes when she rests that I intuit the pose that will best suit her, and then I become the slave of that pose." Strange bondage language. Stranger still, his cold discarding: "I often keep those girls several years, until my interest is exhausted. My plastic signs probably express their souls (a word I dislike), which interests me subconsciously, but what else is there?"

Lydia recognized that Matisse "needed the exaltation with which he responded to the sight and proximity of flowers, brightly colored materials, juicy fruit and the female body which he was going to attempt to sublimate." His manner of working, from the model's point of view, was in-your-face: "His easel almost on top of his subject, he generally painted seated within two meters of the latter as if to be immersed in its atmosphere."

On one occasion a visitor, M. A. Courturier, suggested that Matisse appeared to be "upset" as he approached the canvas. Matisse retorted, "I'm not upset, I'm scared." The studio, according to Courturier, had "an operating room atmosphere, Lydia holding the instruments, a bottle of India ink, the papers, arranging the adjustable table. And Matisse: not a word, drawing, without the slightest sign of agitation, but in this immobility an extreme tension."

"This line of work which demands an air of self-confidence," Lydia writes in her brief memoir essay that accompanies her book *With Apparent Ease . . . Henri Matisse,* "was true drudgery for me." Her book, thanks to photographs Matisse gave her and comments he allowed her to record, documents the painting of herself as *Large Reclining Nude,* in 1935.

Known more familiarly as *The Pink Nude,* it was purchased by the Baltimore collectors Claribel and Etta Cone, the maiden sisters who were arguably the greatest collectors of Matisse, preserving his long history along with several generations of collectors in Europe and America. *The Pink Nude* hangs in the Baltimore Museum of Art, and is Matisse's culminating odalisque.

It wasn't the final lounging woman he ever painted. But in this sculptural figure, cast upon the simple lattice of a royal blue and white checked background, Matisse embodied the fullness he had looked for in the intricacy of Persian carpets, in the woven mysteries of silk and the spun patterns of cobweb lawn. All his "patterns," the arabesques he saw as the fluid, living rhythm art captures on canvas are finally released into the female body.

In 1907 Picasso, seeing Matisse's early *Blue Nude* at Gertrude Stein's apartment, had objected: "If he wants to make a woman, let him make a woman. If he wants to make a design, let him make a design. This is between the two." It was the vexed response of a younger man, looking for categories (not something we associate with Picasso). But for Matisse the interior was a metaphor he could not ignore. He had to paint his way through it to the figure. For the interior, all that festering wallpaper and billowing textile, was the world. Our place.

Now, finally, in *The Pink Nude,* background becomes pure grid, rectilinear, without flower, without curve, a telegraphy of straight lines, the simple squares of abstraction. The odalisque herself possesses the joyous, liberating arabesque, the lifeline that once belonged to the walls and hangings of her chamber. She has drawn into herself all of it— flowers and fruits, all the curvilinear satisfaction of just being-here-now, of being alive.

She is not, after all, an intimate figure, not indolent and domestic. Cast upon the abstract latitudinal/longitudinal lines of her global background, she proves to be a monumental presence. Finally, painting Lydia Delectorskaya, a model who was "not his type," Matisse got the goddess. His odalisque had come to stay. She was there to do the heavy lifting.

Matisse and Delectorskaya lived above the Mediterranean, in Nice and later, during the war and after, in the little town of Vence, working, working in the blissful light until the end came.

OF THE THREE great "sky-god religions" as Gore Vidal calls the religions of Abraham, only one has remained loyal to the first imaginings of their common ur-metaphor: the garden with its streams and fountains, its flowering fruits and vegetables, the docile animals of the peaceable Kingdom. This is the paradise that Islam apparently has never abandoned in its poetry. The youngest of the monotheistic religions steadfastly clings to its central metaphor, the dream-enclosure surrounding the seraglio, the baths, the sensuous life of the body-soul known as human life.

While Judaism and Christianity also enshrine the creation-myth garden metaphor, they stray from it theologically and poetically as Islam does not seem tempted to do. Whatever the reason, religious Judaism does not dream of a domestic garden as its destination (even if the early Zionists were determined "to make the desert bloom"). Judaism dreams of Jerusalem. Its dearest metaphor is the sacred City.

As for Christianity—it long ago traded in its garden for an eternal governmental unit, the Kingdom. And for the better part of two millennia it did everything possible to reify that metaphor into a political reality—Christendom.

The garden metaphor abides in the very image of the harem's enclosure, the paradise of the domestic park, the bower of bliss: the garden as maquette of the world as it should be, could be. All of this exists in the poetry of Rumi, the Sufi mystic who was the elusive author of vast reservoirs of Persian odes and lyrics, and who also founded the trance-dancing order of Mevlevi dervishes, the "whirling" dervishes. He spent his active years in Konya, a city on the great Anatolian steppe in what is now Turkey. He died there in 1273. A monastery-turned-museum houses his mausoleum, surrounded by a garden.

"Seek sweet syrup from the garden of love"—this is the kind of religious poet he is, shocking and erotic, refusing to let brittle piety smother his shattering experience of divinity. He doesn't mind displaying his heart aflame:

> *Where is a bunch of roses,*
> *if you would be this garden?*
> *Where, one soul's pearly essence*
> *when you're the Sea of God?*

A BROILING DAY in late May, tree roses pumping color, fountain burbling in the formal garden of the museum-monastery, shoes off at the entrance, and then into the dark interior, padding around on threadbare carpets, gazing in the dim light at The Tomb. Feeling, of course, nothing much. The tourist malaise.

It's another of my ardent pilgrimages, seeking *the place where. . . .* Here, perhaps, Rumi composed his ecstatic lover-like religious lyrics beneath the archways of the monastery enclosure, below the minaret's spire. *"The bird of my heart has*

again begun to flutter | the parrot of my soul has begun to chew sugar."
For lines like these I have tromped to what was once
called Asia Minor with several friends, as pilgrimage-beset
as I, to this dusty Anatolian plain. *"The hour is late, the hour is
late, the sun has gone down into the well, the sun of the soul of lovers has
entered the seclusion of God."*

Rumi is a poet by accident, the best way to be a poet, no
doubt. He *has* to write this odd stuff that apparently turns
out to be what people call "poems" because only the
peculiarity of poetry, the bent and broken images, the
glimpses, allow for the ducking and leaping, the lunging
and feinting, he must perform to express all his feeling, as
Matisse said of what it is to try to give testimony of the
experience of living in the world.

But Rumi is trying to render the non-world. The mystical transcendence of being. God, in other words. The encounter with That-Which-Is. This task, however, puts
him in yet deeper relation with the world. And poetry
writing, all this trafficking in language, only causes him to
realize his subject is its opposite. He sometimes signs his
poems as Klamush — the Silent:

Silence! Go sauntering through the meadow for today it is
The turn for the eyes to behold. . . .

Choose that dessert which augments life, seek that wine which
Is full-bodied;
The rest is all scent and image and colour, the rest is all war
And shame and opprobrium;
Be silent, and sit down, for you are drunk, and this is the edge
Of the roof.

WE HAVE ONLY a single night in Konya. The hotel is a good one, which is to say there are a lot of mirrors and crystal chandeliers, a spiral staircase with a gilded railing, an absurdly loaded buffet table in a massive dining room. Our little group of five combs the buffet, piling on the creamy eggplant, the lamb kebabs, the cucumbers and tomatoes, the little fried whatever-they-are. We complain that there is too much food, but we go back for the chicken with mint yogurt, and ask for glasses of the salty sour-milk beverage that has become a low-grade addiction. Finally, the "sherbets and fruits" that couldn't appease Delacroix, do, after all, satisfy us.

There is a rare chance, we discover, to see the dervishes perform. Except we are not to think of it as a performance. We are not to clap. This is the Sema, a ritual dance, a religious rite. The hotel has provided the Mevlevi order with a private area in the basement with a small dance floor (obviously set up at other times for a band). We file downstairs with another group, Japanese tourists who bow to us. They have been told not to take photographs, but they cannot help themselves, and during the first few minutes, as the dervishes file in, the snapping is quite intense.

We are seated around the little parquet dance floor. The men wear loose white soutanes, except for one, the dance master, who is in black. On their heads, upside-down bucket hats, also white. The white gowns are the ego's burial shroud. The toques on their heads are the ego's tombstones. Several other men, in black, are the musicians, playing reed and string instruments and a drumlike object. Two singers settle in with them against the wall.

I expect the dancing to become a frenzy, a wild-and-crazy ecstatic loss of control. But the stately turning never speeds up madly. The whirling is the soft insistence of billowing water lilies opening on the dark surface of the dance floor's shiny water. They go around and around, in some hermetic pattern of their own hypnotic rhythm. There is nothing virtuosic about the dancing, and yet the dignity of it is compelling, demanding even. Their hats, for some reason, do not look silly. They *need* the hats. They are part of the dance. Well, they are their tombstones. Even the Japanese have settled down, cameras no longer snapping. We simply stare. Our eyes follow the billowing skirts of the solemn men as they turn, turn.

At some point they become fish moving in water. The movement is no longer happening from their feet. They are mermen moving in the dark dance-floor air that has become water. It is impossible to stay awake. The ease is so overpowering my head lolls forward. I'm not exactly asleep. I'm just limp, watching the white garments swirl, swirling with them as I sit in one of the straight-backed chairs ringing the seedy dance floor. And that is how it is until—when? an hour later? longer?—the white waterlily men, the mermen, move in formation, a school of fish, off the little hotel dance floor into the back room from which they first emerged, and it seems that all of this might never have occurred or that it might have been happening for a long time, much longer than anyone would believe.

Then, perhaps because it is all a little disorienting and it is impossible to think of going to the bar for a drink, everyone goes upstairs to bed, overtaken with a kind of floating exhaustion. But I have seen a sign—BATHS—on a door and I'm determined to take advantage of the chance, the first time on our two-week trip a Turkish bath has been offered. No one will go with me—but finally Susan agrees, the redhead who knows I'm afraid to open the door and enter alone the room next to the one where the dervishes danced that is marked BATHS.

We are met by a barrel-chested, mustachioed man, sent by Central Casting for a Monty Python version of *The Arabian Nights.* He's wearing a small red towel tucked around his shiny, bulging midsection. And nothing else. His feet slap on the wet floor, his hairy shoulders gleam with the damp of the place, as if he worked, like the night watchman of my father's greenhouse, in a hellish cauldron of heat. His bald head wrinkles with the smiles that start at his face, rippling upward. He looks like a man who would have a substantial harem.

He leads us to separate stalls to undress and gives each of us a skimpy towel. Then we are to go into the sauna, step one. We sit there, just the two of us, sweating in the cedar, throwing water on the hot rocks, our lungs seizing on the steam. I feel a kind of miserable desperation — why am I doing this? — and I realize Susan is the only friend I have in all the world. I've left my glasses in the dressing room, and the world is not only steamy, but terribly imprecise, wavering. The beginning of a bad dream.

A rap on the sauna door, and we look at each other, clutch our thin towels, and emerge. Then we are scrubbed . . . within an inch of our lives. Susan first. I see strange narrow gray ropes forming on her back and slipping away under the corrugated rubber mitt of the mustachioed sultan. It takes me a while to understand this is *skin.* The same happens to me, the outer layer flayed, even the heels rounded off and made new.

He has tried to speak to us, but he doesn't know a word

of English—not many English come here. We can say hello and thank you in Turkish, and he rewards us with an alarming smile, his bald head crinkling. He knows some Japanese—Do we know Japanese? Ah, too bad— he makes this gesture. Many Japanese, he mimes, holding his hands to his face, making clicking sounds with his invisible camera.

We are shampooed and lathered, washed and rinsed, pails of water sluiced and gushed over us. Susan looks like a rosy goddess, laid out on the round marble slab in the middle of the room. Out of a pillowcase (it looks like) dipped again and again into a bucket of milky water, the burly man casts a down comforter of suds over her until she is entirely covered, as if for night, under a duvet of dense bubbles. Then he massages her body, working with one leg up on the marble, knee bent, hard at it, giving her shoulder an impersonal little slap when it is time to turn, to move, to get up.

Then my turn. Under my blanket of bubbles I lie content, spent without having done a thing, cast upon the warmed marble, my body broken of its vertical, the arabesque of ease pounded into me. Then a sharp rap on my shoulder, and I rise on one arm, leg extended, the marble room whirling with steam and myopia. Susan is a lolling rose nearby, a girlfriend talking about what constitutes a good manicure—and did I know that the root for the word *cosmetics* is "cosmos." Think about it, she says, swigging mineral water from a plastic bottle, the petals of her body open, blushing with color.

We stay like this for a while, long minutes swooning in the warm fog. The Turkish bath man, off duty now, regards his handiwork. He turns the little water sluicing pail upside down on his head, and begins moving, round and round, slowly on his delicate dancing feet, a pudgy cartoon dervish, whirling around the marble plinth on which we lie. Then he stops before me, offers his arm to lead me back to the little dressing room where—is it hours ago?—I left the tokens of my other life. He knows I cannot be trusted to walk upright alone. I lean into him, feeling deliciously collapsible. This night I'm an odalisque at last, all fish, all float.

SIX

Balcony

The Côte d'Azur. The ultramarine basin of what used to be called Western Civilization. In Marseille, twelve miles from Jerome Hill's house in Cassis, a bronze medallion is embedded into the cement at the edge of the old port where fishermen still dock to sell their catch from the back of their boats, but where the real business is tourism. *Ici,* it proclaims, exactly *here,* 2,600 centuries ago, Phocian traders arrived from Asia Minor and established Civilization — hauling it in tow, apparently, a commodity much in demand. From this spot, the medallion reads, Civilization *radiated* across the world.

You have to love the French—*Ici* and nowhere else. Still able to think of "Civilization" as singular—and theirs to dole out. There was considerable consternation several years ago when archaeologists determined that the ancient port, long silted in, had, in fact, been several blocks away from the current *vieux port.* The *Ici,* it turned out, was actually *Là-bas.* For a while the question of removing the plaque to this more accurate, though less touristic, site was a matter of civic debate.

For inspiration-idolators as well as sun-and-light seekers keep coming generation after generation to this ridge of the Mediterranean running roughly from Marseille all the way to Nice and Menton, riveted the whole length with gleaming villages and towns. I've come here, too, to Cassis, looking, like everybody else, for inspiration. That's what it means to seek a place apart, especially a beautiful, exalted place. My plan: to sit here for a few months, write some short stories, head back to Minnesota, my northern place and my fate, where I will—what else?—write more stories, possibly better ones, at least probably not worse ones.

The inspiration artists seek is surely not all a matter of location location location, but there must be a reason why artists and writers keep wandering about, seeking the Right Place. And why generations have come here to this string of towns facing across the great blue to the rim of Africa: for inspiration, we say—or don't say, but secretly think.

It's strange that we still believe in inspiration when, compared to earlier ages, we seem to believe in so little. Inspiration may be the one bit of God we haven't managed to kill off. The big bearded Primary Cause and his timepiece may have stopped ticking for us, Jesus may have become "historical," but the Holy Ghost is still aloft.

Even rigorous atheists speak easily of what "inspires" them—presumably this is not just a figure of speech but an attempt to describe a galvanizing, unbidden inner impulse. And while many people are careful to make clear they have no time for "organized religion," they attest fervently to the importance of their "spiritual life." Spirit exists, in other words. It continues to go about its primordial job: to breathe its mystery into our fiber so that we might breathe out the bit of meaning it entrusts to us.

But these gustings are idiosyncratic, personal, often a bit nutty. They are as impossible (or boring) to recite (or rather, to listen to) as a dreamer's breakfast-table attempt to convey the numinous power of the night's dream. These romantic inner-inspirations only come alive in translation—in a story, a poem, a picture. Such inspiration, romantic and real, is everywhere, not just, or not especially, here, along this glittering coast where, for ages, so many have made pilgrimage and even made their home, at least for a lucky while.

But a more antique form of inspiration haunts this Provençal place and has brought me here, I think. Or has presented itself now that I am here. This older inspiration is the austere classical cousin of the wild Romantic not-I-but-the-wind inspiration I have always trusted, with its passionate commitment to Henry James's "rich principle of the Note," the Romantic habit of personal attention and naming, Matisse's attempt to "convey all his emotion" in response to experience.

This older piety of the ancients was rooted in a reverence for ancestors, an instinct to bow the head to those who preceded, who lived, worked, loved, and sometimes died along this curve of the Mediterranean, first colonized well before the birth of Christ by the Romans who brought here the gnarled grapevine and the silver olive.

Theirs was not the Christian piety of personal do-gooding, but the placement of the small self in relation to history.

But what is to be gained by lighting a taper before a shrine, any shrine, sacred or secular?

An accurate gauge of one's own smallness, for one thing. And paradoxically, an intense sensation of companionship, of kinship with—and now, rounding the corner, comes the word that won't be denied—with *greatness.* "You and your four-bit words," my modest father, toiling in his northern greenhouse, used to say. But he smiled. He believed in the four-bit words, too. Not the greatness of individual accomplishment, but the grandeur of endeavor, the splendor of the attempt that links immortals to amateurs, from age to age, and finally latches on to the inspiring impersonality of history itself.

I speed along the autoroute to take advantage of the deals at Auchan, the *hypermarché* spread out, as such places are everywhere, in a massive commercial plain dislocated from anything but itself. I am living, for these lucky months, along a filet of real estate that is now so valuable no artist seeking to revolutionize the world's eyesight (Matisse figuring out fauvism in 1904 at Saint-Tropez, in

Collioure in 1905) could afford to rent a view here. No consumptive English short-story writer (Katherine Mansfield after the First World War) would find her Villa Isola Bella available (with garden and housekeeper) on a hillside overlooking the sea for so many guineas a year.

But they came here, so many of my saints—Mansfield first to Cassis, then to Bandol and Menton; Fitzgerald with the Murphys near Antibes; Ford Maddox Ford meandering through Provence; Sybille Bedford as a girl with her bohemian mother to Sanary-sur-Mer, followed there after 1933 by a clutch of Nazi-fleeing German writers—Thomas Mann, Franz Werfel, Bertolt Brecht. Even Virginia Woolf spent a string of summers lured by her sister Vanessa's idolatry of the sun to little Cassis, where I sit now (view of Med) drinking a cup of linden-flower tea (an inadvertent *hommage à Proust* who did *not* come here). I'm following them—they formed the century that formed me.

Whatever inspiration radiates from the bronze plaque in its almost correct location in Marseille belonged first to the pagan world to which this place ever reverts, rooted deep in its Roman vines and olives. It is the inspiration that comes from contemplating not oneself or one's own bit of news. This is the inspiration that abides in the contemplation of the greatness of others, their sacrifice, their terrible blindness and tragic missteps, their refusal to disappear after they have disappeared.

Tradition, Chesterton said, is the democracy of the dead. The ancients believed in the dead, their enduring presence. They worshipped the dead. And why not? The dead are all around us, and maybe here, along this coastal range with its ultramarine light, the membrane separating us from us is just slightly more porous. Perhaps they wish to be of use, still.

Of all of them, I first chose for my pagan saint Katherine Mansfield. She might have been for me, as she probably is for most readers, one of the usual suspects rounded up in the anthologies, represented by her "perfect" short story, "The Garden Party." Beyond this cameo, she might have receded into that twilight where minor writers refuse to be extinguished entirely, trailing clouds of her "exquisite" sensibility, the unfulfilled promise of her talent excused by her tragic early death.

She might have surfaced again in the biographies of her more celebrated friends: Virginia Woolf, who saw in her a rival, and D. H. Lawrence, who used her as the model for Gudrun in *Women in Love.* She might have seemed that kind of filmy background figure—if I had come to her through her fiction.

But I read Mansfield's *Journal* and *Letters* first, documents pulsing with the ardent confusion of art and life that I was just beginning to scramble up myself. "I want to *work*," she confided to her journal

> . . . so to live that I work with my hands and my feeling and my brain. I want a garden, a small house, grass, animals, books, pictures, music. And out of this, the expression of this, I want to be writing. (Though I may write about cabmen. That's no matter.)
>
> But warm, eager, living life—to be rooted in life—to learn, to desire to know, to feel, to think, to act. That is what I want.

She articulated for me what it was to want to *be* a writer—and against heavy odds.

But even the autobiographical intimacy of those personal forms—journals and letters—doesn't explain the fascination I developed for Mansfield in my teens that persisted into my twenties. The word *fascination* hardly states the case. For years, in college and graduate school, and beyond that through the series of dumb jobs and frequent moves I made from one crummy apartment to another as I, too, tried "to be a writer," home was where I hammered a nail and hung the stark photograph of Mansfield's hieratic consumptive face. My shrine, my saint.

I read everybody with fierce appetite during those years—Whitman, Virginia Woolf, Lawrence, poets beyond count. I had many heroes. But I didn't just read Mansfield. I stalked her. I tracked any shred of memory or gossip. When I found in Frieda Lawrence's memoir that, during the period when they had lived next door in Cornwall, Mansfield had introduced her to Cuticura soap, I was off to Walgreens, thrilled to find that in 1968 it was still possible to buy the assertive clove-scented bar. A relic.

I learned from one of her biographers (for a supposedly minor writer, she had quite a few) that Mansfield liked to keep "low bowls of bright flowers" on her writing table:

I affected the same, and as a florist's daughter, approved the gesture. She favored—again, according to Frieda Lawrence who could be counted on for girl talk—little jackets of "lovely colours and soft velvet materials": soon my style as well, though my latter-day velvets draped over faded jeans. Mine was the moist devotion of a cultist, not the frank pleasure of a reader.

Of course I also read the short stories. I approved her pitch-perfect ear for a volley of dialogue, the click of her snapshot scenes. Her descriptive delight in the world winked with bright, effortless figures. "After lunch today," she wrote from Menton, "we had a sudden tremendous thunderstorm, the drops of rain were as big as marguerite daisies—the whole sky was violet. I went out the very moment it was over—the sky was all glittering with broken light—the sun a huge splash of silver. The drops were like silver fishes hanging from the tree."

The voice in my favorite stories ("Prelude," "At the Bay") combines cool authority with an unspoken, and therefore all the more convincing, heartache for her lost New Zealand. I knew that her Wellington had hardly been cherished at the time (no more had I cherished

St. Paul). Like me, she knew she was a provincial, and she longed to escape—and did, to London in 1908, before she was twenty. But successful nostalgia is bred of regret, and Katherine Mansfield was a great regretter. After her relatively brief wild-thing period, illness turned her into a pondering, sometimes frantic, invalid. Her gleeful escape was twisted into lonely exile.

Her fiction spoke to me in a less personal voice than the urgent manner of the *Journal* and *Letters,* but this too is evidence of her particular genius: Mansfield was a writer who could bare her soul *and* write with detached authority. She exposed the membrane between self and art, the porous fiber that transformed a raw girlish ambition and overheated poeticism into the remorseless assurance of fiction.

Why were there no novels? I wondered briefly, but even this lack turned into virtue: Katherine Mansfield was a miniaturist, not a big-sweep writer, but all the finer for that, a noticer of gestures, a tender of oblique details, capable of the occasional well-aimed dart. She fretted about this: "Don't I live in *glimpses only*?" she writes in a letter. But she also understood that her idea of a story's form was genuinely new, *"pure risk,"* as she said, moving not by plot but by impression and association, episodes strung on a brief string of time. Her vision was essentially poetic, not narrative, and this enlivened her voice, and for me, her appeal.

The condensed spirit of the penciled note gave her work a striking immediacy. For all her intensity, she was not a fainter and swooner. She was modern and proud of it. Her humor was mordant, even unkind. Her lyricism had a squeeze of lemon to it.

Virginia Woolf might write to her sister in an initial assessment of Mansfield, that she found her "cheap and hard . . . unscrupulous." But Mansfield possessed the keener eye for character, writing to Ottoline Morrell after this first meeting that she sensed in Woolf "the strange, trembling, glinting quality of her mind . . . she seemed to me to be one of those Dostoevsky women whose 'innocence' has been hurt."

Mansfield suffered—this, too, was important to me. As with Keats, everywhere and never forgotten, even in her most rhapsodic flights, her youthful death hovered. No wonder there were no novels. She died at thirty-four, after years of suffering from tuberculosis.

But unlike Virginia Woolf or Sylvia Plath (the afflicted women writers my friends favored), Mansfield's tubercular lungs were bursting to live, live. My saint might die, but extinguish herself? Never. Would Chekhov have killed himself? And Chekhov, I learned from the critics (including Mansfield's own husband—and arch-promoter—John Middleton Murry) was the writer Mansfield most resembled. She translated, with a Russian friend, some of the earliest Chekhov stories to be published in English. A scandal stewed for decades after her death: had she plagiarized a Chekhov story, passing it off as her own in the very early years before he was much known to English readers? Her accusers and defenders hurled their darts in the *Times Literary Supplement* for half a century after her death.

She really resembled more truly Jean Rhys (Mansfield nailed "the woman alone" theme before Rhys got to it). Even more fundamentally, Colette was her kin. Like Colette, Mansfield had her youthful cabaret period, complete with club performances and lesbian flirtations, and though she wrote of the first generation of urban "free" women, her sensuous evocations of nature were her signature. Had she lived, she might have made a very likely

English Colette, an earthier mother-of-us-all than Virginia Woolf.

The *Journal* and the *Letters* were suffused with consumptive ecstasy. She saw it in Lawrence: "I recognized his smile—just the least shade too bright . . . his air of being a touch more vividly alive than other people—the gleam." Her "work," as she wrote of it in the *Journal*, became a kind of parallel universe, spiritualized, even sacralized as the clock ran out. She spoke severely of "sinning against art." This, too, I reverenced: the religion of art.

Keats was *her* saint. She wrote of him in her journal as of a colleague. Keats, in turn, had his heroes: he lugged around a portrait of Shakespeare wherever he lived—another young writer given to hero worship. I perceived—or created—of this relationship a lineage that lifted Mansfield out of the cramped quarters where she lodged in the rented rooms of the anthologists. Boldly (if privately) I attached her to the great Romantic dynasty as expressly configured by and for me: Shakespeare to Keats to Mansfield. She may have been the Pygmalion of the bunch, but I dragooned her into the firmament.

And who was going to stop me? It was the early seventies, and we were supposed to be "discovering" women writers, wedging them into the literary canon any which way. Yet it is strange that I fastened on Mansfield. Virginia Woolf, whose novels I read at the time, and admired, did not compel me to rush off to buy her brand of face soap. Mansfield was my girl. But then, I didn't "discover" her. She had been willed to me.

I MUST HAVE BEEN about seventeen when Doris Derman turned to me in her majestic old St. Paul apartment just off Summit Avenue (a few blocks west of Jerome Hill's boyhood house and a few blocks east of "the house below the average on a street above the average," as Fitzgerald described his parents' home where he learned Scribners would publish *This Side of Paradise*). She was standing in the shadowy living room, having just taken her martini from her husband when she said, in response to something I had said and which I have now entirely forgotten, "That is the sort of observation Katherine Mansfield made."

I had never heard of Katherine Mansfield; for a moment I thought Doris was referring to a friend of hers. In any case, Doris Derman, worldly mother of my first boy-friend, was willing to make the introduction. "You may have these," she said, and walked over to her ceiling-high bookcase (itself an essential prop of the life I hoped to enter: the life of the mind) and handed me two books, one bound in faded orange linen with a yet-more-faded green spine, the other in a sad blue with dull silver lettering. The orange, its title stamped in worn gold, was the *Letters,* the blue was the *Journal.*

It is hard to convey how stunned I was that such personal writings had been *published.* Stories, novels, poems— these were the stuff of books—weren't they? But letters, diaries—I wrote them myself; I never imagined they could be "literature."

Doris Derman was the first person, besides a teacher, I heard speak with authority about books and writers. But her authority was different; she spoke not from a height but from within the precinct of the initiated. She had opinions, and they were based on nothing but her own taste and whim. Such brashness was unheard of in my convent-school world of hierarchy and certainty where references to authority were—authoritative.

Living in the same neighborhood, in the same parish (as Catholic St. Paul referenced all civic boundaries), Doris knew my family, knew who I was and from whence I came. But we had never met until her son brought me home. He had artlessly confessed that his mother had told him before this meeting, "Beware of a girl whose family believes the world is no bigger than Linwood Avenue between Lexington and Oxford." Our block.

I wasn't hurt by this tart dismissal that, of course, I was not intended to hear. In fact, I approved. It confirmed my own readiness to dismiss St. Paul and its careful Catholic ways that battened me far more (I later thought) than Katherine Mansfield's stodgy Wellington had ever squashed her.

But more than that: I was subtly thrilled that Doris had *captured* us, had summed us up—had *written* us, in effect. My family did not talk this way, did not think this way. The hauteur necessary to make such a remark, the aerial aloofness from—well, from Linwood between Lexington and Oxford—would have given my family nosebleeds. Doris's cool ability to consign us to the higher world of description—to fiction, really—won me even before I met her.

Though her husband was Catholic and, of course, her son was also, Doris was alluringly non-Catholic. She dyed her hair a blatant, unapologetic blond, and I understood she had once "written." There was the definite sense that as someone who *had written,* she was in possession of talent, vast sums she held prudently in ethereal escrow.

She was a good ten years older than the other mothers in the parish and she appeared to take no interest in doing her share at school functions. She let her husband handle the grocery shopping, all driving, any necessary encounters with nuns and teachers. He was a gentle man who seemed conscripted to serve her, nervously asking, as he handed her a drink he had mixed in the kitchen while she lay, stretched out on the couch reading in the shadowy living room, whether she felt all right. Heaven knew what she did on Sunday mornings when the rest of us were at St. Luke's for Mass. She wasn't simply a non-Catholic. It appeared she was not religious at all, perhaps an agnostic.

This was all good, good news.

I can't think of Katherine Mansfield without conjuring Doris Derman—not because she entrusted her books to me and set me on the particular literary path—favoring clarity and immediacy, the bittersweet but fundamentally comic point of view—that I still think of as the high road. Not even because she introduced me to "the personal voice" in literature when she handed me Mansfield's *Journal* and *Letters,* thus opening the door to memoir and the personal essay, forms I came to prize and practice. It's simply that, over the years, her passion for Mansfield has become more eloquent to me than my own strenuous teen-idol feelings.

Mansfield was the doomed artist for Doris's generation. Make that the doomed *woman* artist. In a sense, Mansfield was this earlier generation's version of Sylvia Plath. Or, to put it in the proper chronology, Plath was my generation's version of Mansfield: the exemplary figure who combined talent, youth, beauty, passion, drive—and death. Early death.

This is why Virginia Woolf, who committed suicide at fifty-nine, doesn't quite figure in this equation. The exemplary figure of the doomed artist must be one extinguished before endeavor has fully transmitted itself into achievement. Death is the massive gilt frame that pulls the eye away from the work. But that's the point: with certain writers it is impossible (and for Doris, undesirable) to separate the two. Doris was mesmerized not by the flicker of Mansfield's talent but by the extinguished light, the burnt wick.

Doris pondered all sides of the story, the glory of the bold escape from the provinces, the sexual high jinks (Mansfield was representative of the world's first generation of "free women"), the brilliant lyric sensibility, the desperate final mysticism. The long consumptive death following on the heels of this sexually gallant youth conveyed metaphorically (that is, effectively) for Doris's generation the terrible odds against a woman of talent and ambition.

Mansfield's work and life, taken together, enshrined the fineness of her talent and the punishment that came of the attempt to live the "free life" that she assumed was essential to the work. It was what a later generation of women would call a liberated life. And you got hammered for it.

Fundamentally, Doris's fascination with Mansfield had to do with what it revealed about the catastrophic result of the attempt to be free. Better to "have written" sometime briefly in the past, better to sock your talent safely away. Stay high in the shadowy apartment on Summit

Avenue, keep your hair glamour-bright, accept another drink from your hovering husband.

Mansfield's death — coming, literally, out of the air — spoke forcefully to Doris's generation of the implacable forces arrayed against the gallant woman. The final massive hemorrhage, at the Gurdjieff community near Fontainebleau where she had gone to "purify" herself, bespoke the barely grasped independence of the "new woman" and the dismal fate that awaited her for stepping outside the assigned circle of safety.

Just so, several decades later, after another world war, and much else (including the development of drugs to cure TB), a later generation fastened on to the work and suicide of Sylvia Plath to express an otherwise inexpressible aspect of their sense of things. Plath's suicide, her *choice* of death, appears to be the opposite of Mansfield's frantic dash, from French seaside to alpine chalet, from doctors to quacks, finally to a proto–New Age guru, to save herself by any means. Yet they shared an emblematic power.

Doris was a teenager when Mansfield died in 1923. Doris belonged to the generation that had just inherited the short skirts and bold bobbed haircuts that Mansfield, for one, made the daring symbol of the new woman. For Doris she was a tantalizing bohemian big sister. She'd been up to no good, and look what happened: sick, alone, exiled, dead. Her slim oeuvre was dwarfed by the journals and the passionate correspondence bred of terrible loneliness in which she alternately bemoaned her fate and shored up her courage and ever-dimming hopes with crystalline descriptions of the world about her. They are among the great letters in English literature, fairly compared to the letters of Keats.

It may be a gloomy commentary on my generation that we chose as our exemplary figure a suicide. In Mansfield, Doris chose a figure on whom the fates descended, but whose pact with life itself not only remained unbroken, but was cranked up to an almost excruciating pitch of desire and attachment.

In Plath, on the other hand, my generation chose a model of brilliant sourness, a woman whose fury was finally directed at life itself, not at its cruel refusal to admit her and sustain her. Even if she was exemplary because we *didn't* want to follow her, Plath was the lost woman writer who came to haunt us, as Mansfield haunted Doris Derman. But with this difference: Doris, I think, felt companioned by Mansfield. In spite of everything, she was a benign ghost.

Mansfield's cool talent and her desperado life were indelibly bonded, if they had not been before, by Murry's publication of the *Journal* in 1927, just four years after her death. The *Letters* followed swiftly in 1928. Although Mansfield knew a measure of literary, if not truly popular, fame in her lifetime, her appeal really hit its international stride as a result of Murry's decision to fashion out of her voluminous personal writing books that made her the figure who could take, as he gushingly said, "her rightful place as the most wonderful writer and most beautiful spirit of our time."

As a disgusted friend remarked at the time, Murry was "boiling Katherine's bones to make soup."

Doris did not see it this way—and of course neither did I. We believed in books. We spoke of them as of people whose integrity was above reproach, not objects fashioned and formed. We revered the final rhapsodic line of the *Journal*—*"All is well."* We took the italics to heart and read them as a final triumphant testament. *All is well.*

Ah! Doris and I said, bowing our heads before the courageous farewell of our heroine. *Ah!*

NOW, ALL THESE years later, I've been given an apartment for four months in Cassis, a writing fellowship at Jerome Hill's foundation—the sort of improbable postmodern perk that would have astonished Mansfield in her fruitless search for a safety net.

I've come to Bandol on a day trip from Cassis with two new friends (Susan, an Englishwoman, and her Danish husband, Steffen). We passed east through La Ciotat, the town Jerome Hill featured in his film autobiography, paying homage to the Lumière brothers' first film clip ever shown in a movie house, the train engine pulling into the La Ciotat station. And now we're here, in Mansfield's Bandol, as I think of it, as if she owned it, this quiet Mediterranean fishing village in her day, a bright tourist town in ours.

This trip is an unabashed pilgrimage, though my days as a cultist are over. Here, during separate visits, Mansfield wrote "Prelude" and "Bliss," which I have just reread and have urged on my new friends, glad the stories still seem fresh, glad to spread the word, as Doris once passed it to me. I have also reread the letters. But their magic has turned dark. Gone, the old thrill of exalted sensibility, the breathless lyric acuity trained on raindrops. Gone the romantic scrim that allowed me to ignore, in my poeticism, what it was all about: utter terror of the death bearing down on her.

We are looking for the place where Mansfield wrote "Bliss," the Hôtel Beau Rivage, a name so evocative it sounds like the name of a hotel *in* a story rather than a hotel where a story was written. It is a beautiful day, still winter, as people here insist, though as a Minnesotan I know this is nonsense, and we are deep into spring, trees blossoming, tables set out for lunch, sailboats groaning companionably in their slips.

We have one of those lunches they write about in magazines, timeless and winey. There is crème brûlée, quivering under burnt sugar in a fluted glass dish, and little cups of bitter coffee to set you straight at the end of the meal.

We walk up the street to the hotel, a great peachy Belle Époque business; the grounds are parklike, gracious. A very small old man out of a cautionary fairy tale is pruning, with scissors far too big for him, an immense wisteria vine covering an entire wall. The vine's main branch, espaliered against the stone, is thick as a tree. The scent is overpowering.

The old man smiles at my request—he has heard this before—and silently leads us through the grounds to the hotel entrance where we are handed over to a likewise diminutive old woman, his mate or his colleague. She points to the plaque mounted in the vestibule. In French it says: THREE HOURS AGO I FINISHED MY STORY "BLISS." THANK GOD I HAD GREAT HAPPINESS IN THE WRITING OF IT.

The small woman nods as the old man did, ready to accommodate: yes, I may go up to see the Room. So up the little *ascenseur* we go, the little woman, Susan, Steffen, and I. On the top (third) floor, there it is—the door open (all the doors of all the rooms are open, waiting for their nonexistent occupants: we never see a single guest or tenant). The room is now a double, as it was not in 1918. Appliances are lined up along one wall for a kitchen.

It's not exactly seedy, not even tacky, just honestly, seriously worn. The place was probably lovely in its day, but has been redone, it appears, in the miserable fifties, left to pickle in its unhealthy browns and beiges, its sickish greens. But oddly, the very cheapness of the veneers, the "modern" furniture sighing with shabbiness—all of it enshrines the life of hired rooms and not much money: her life.

The little woman nods—I may open the french doors, may step out on the balcony. Then I'm in the air, looking out, as she must have looked when she rose from her table, having had her three hours of "happiness in the writing." So here it is: the same thrilling sea (more boats, more people, more everything, but the same blue, the same exalted height). "She took the best room," the tiny old woman at my side murmurs, as if to say we all know how Katherine would, of course, take the best.

"KATHERINE HAS BEEN DEAD a week," Virginia Woolf wrote in her diary after the news came from France:

At that one feels—what? A shock of relief?—a rival the less? Then confusion at feeling so little—then, gradually, blankness & disappointment; then a depression which I could not rouse myself from all that day. When I began to write, it seemed to me there was no point in writing. Katherine wont read it. Katherine's my rival no longer. . . . Still there are things about writing I think of & want to tell Katherine. . . . And I was jealous of her writing— the only writing I have ever been jealous of.

It was sometime in the late 1980s that I read this rawly honest passage. Woolf's *Diaries* were being published; the biographies were coming thick and fast. There was more about Mansfield as well. It turned out, according to a carefully sleuthed biography by Claire Tomalin, that although Mansfield had indeed died of TB, it was undiagnosed gonorrhea, contracted during her first year of "freedom," that had weakened her and left her fatally vulnerable.

So much for freedom. Even the *All is well* finale of the *Journal* proved to be a bit of stagecraft—Middleton Murry's. He had not simply edited the *Journal*—he had orchestrated it, piecing bits together to form a narrative that ended with this "triumph" of the spirit.

But Doris was long gone by the time I was reading the postcult biographies. My mother, still living in the neighborhood, had reported that people first noticed that the milkman (the milkman!) was showing up later and later on his rounds. Drinking at the Dermans', was the word. Dead drunk at 10:00 AM, according to the woman at the drugstore. Also: seen wandering on Grand Avenue, thinning blond hair in disarray, wearing bathroom slippers in the snow.

Then, not seen at all, spending all her time in the dark, the blinds pulled, not even sobering up when her husband came home, the children grown and well out of it by now. Finally, sprawled on the bathroom floor, "found" by her husband when he came home from work downtown.

We had read the last line of the *Journal* as a personal message, almost a directive. *All is well.* We stayed with Mansfield to the end, past the little pleasures of tea at the Villa Isola Bella in lemon-sunny Menton where she wrote some of her best late stories. We followed her to the thin air of Sierre high in the Alps, past her furious marital disappointment in Murry. Doris made short work of him: "A drip, obviously," she said. We stayed with Katherine (as we called her) right to the moment she entered the weird community at Fontainebleau to be purified by the Master, and died her gasping, operatic death after running up a flight of steps. "She was so happy," Doris said, as if she had been there. "She forgot to be careful."

Still, *all was well.* Katherine had said so. Doris never had reason to disbelieve her testimony. Or maybe Doris kept to herself just how well she thought everything really was. Maybe she didn't wish to disillusion me: maybe she wanted to pass along the literary torch, burning with a "too bright" gleam, but all the same, shedding the only light that mattered to us, what Katherine's rivalrous friend Virginia called "the lamp in the spine," the glow of the imagination powering a life.

My mother saw it more simply. "Doris Derman was a fine woman," she said, as if someone had suggested otherwise. She did not like the gossip about the milkman. "She was a lady. She had talent." Then she paused, searching for what she really meant, what for her was highest praise: "She was a serious reader."

COOKING KATHERINE'S BONES *to make soup . . .*

Ours, of course, is an age with a stronger stomach for raw autobiography. We have also developed a taste for the writer's story behind the story, for what is called "creative process," what Henry James called "the celestial process." Mansfield's notebooks and letters provide fascinating, sometimes heartbreaking, testimony of both her life and her art. Her struggle against loneliness and the ache of abandonment she describes during the years of illness rise beyond personal complaints, and become, in her transparent prose, models of spiritual searching.

Like the letters of Keats and Chekhov that she revered, Mansfield's personal writing is especially eloquent about the artist's attempt to track the most direct route to the imagination against the sweeping tide of personal devastation. She trusted the wisdom of brevity and ellipsis. Chekhov, she felt, "made a mistake in thinking that if he had had more time he would have written more fully, described the rain & the midwife & doctor having tea. The truth is one can get only *so much* into a story; there is always a sacrifice. . . . It's always a kind of race, to get in as much as one can before it *disappears.*"

Finally, no matter his motives, Murry was right: if Mansfield was not "the most wonderful writer" or "most beautiful spirit," she certainly was the most emblematic woman writer of her time. More, even, than Virginia Woolf who envied "the bright sharp-cut circle" of Mansfield's "extraordinarily vivid attention," as Desmond MacCarthy described her style, which left Woolf confessing to her diary, "I was jealous of her writing—the only writing I have ever been jealous of."

Mansfield, six years younger than Woolf, led a reckless bohemian youth, and had nothing of the Bloomsbury bluestocking to her. Her early death and aura of desperation may account for the virtual cult of Katherine that ensued from Murry's publication of her personal writings. But there was—and remains—more to her enduring position in English letters. Mansfield has fairly retained her allure precisely because it has become increasingly difficult to pry her work (the stories) from her life (the notebooks and letters).

Like her adored Keats, Mansfield sought in personal forms—letters, notebook jottings—to reveal the heart of the imaginative enterprise as time closed in upon her.

Her understanding that consciousness itself and what she called "glimpses" were the distinguishing marks of the modern writer has proved to be accurate. "The waves, as I drove home this afternoon," she writes in an undated notebook from one of her Mediterranean residencies, "—and the high foam, how it was suspended in the air before it fell . . . What is it that happens in that moment of suspension? It is timeless. In that moment . . . the whole life of the soul is contained."

For most of the twentieth century Mansfield's "The Garden Party" was taught in English classes as a "perfect" story, included in virtually every anthology of short fiction. If it no longer appears as routinely, perhaps contemporary taste has finally caught up with Mansfield who assessed it coolly in her notebook as "a moderately successful story—and that's all."

Her longer, more atmospheric stories, like "Prelude" and "At the Bay" that recapture her New Zealand childhood, now seem more striking. They form a bridge between the "glimpses" of her notebooks and her "perfect" stories.

In 1915, in the south of France, she dreamed of keeping "a kind of minute notebook—to be published some day.

That is all. No novels, no problem stories, nothing that is not simple, open." In her frail notations from Gurdjieff's Fontainebleau institute, Mansfield is often reduced to painfully eloquent single words and phrases for which she needed the Russian equivalent: "I am cold, bring paper to light a fire . . . wood . . . flame . . . strength . . . light a fire . . . no more fire."

Mansfield seems not to have made a grand last statement—no up-with-the-violins *"All is well"* as Murry had it. She put her faith in captured details, a modernist loyal to captured bits and fragments to the end. "It was an exquisite day," the final paragraph of the *Notebooks* begins. "It was one of those days so clear, so still, so silent you almost feel the earth itself has stopped in astonishment at its own beauty."

She kept up her "minute notebook" even when stories were beyond her. "Unruffled sea," she wrote on the last page of her last notebook. "The gulls moved like the lights within a pearl." It was, perhaps, her final "glimpse."

SEVEN

Chapel

Soon I will leave. Leave the dream space of the sun-and-sea of Cassis, the edge of Europe where the twentieth century tried to imagine a new way of seeing things, of saying things. I'll head back home to St. Paul where by now, early June, the lilacs have rusted away and winter has faded even from memory like one of those vengeful old gods nobody believes in anymore. A strange, amnesiac climate, my north. After months of abusive behavior, the bully winter always slinks off, lost in the sticky aphasia of summer. *I love the change of seasons*—that lunatic

Minnesota remark, delivered to the dismayed faces of the sane in their temperate climates.

In my own "minute notebook," written here in Cassis not far from where Mansfield dreamed of writing hers, all winter and into spring I've taken an escaped northlander's delight in describing the weather, a tally of perfect days, the sun, the sea, daily remarking my escape as if my job were to report from the Other Side.

Even the mistral hasn't been a fright, though people here speak of it solemnly, the ferocious wind blowing from the Alps like a reminder of the truth of things for those malingering, as I have done these sweet months, along the ancient coast where Civilization, according to the bronze plaque in the Marseille port, first risked coming ashore.

I've loved it here—of course. Sitting in the sun by the port, basking in one of the red canvas chairs at M. Brun's ("my" café), ordering *un grand crème,* my market basket by my side, masquerading as a local, sometimes adding the prop of *Le Monde,* which I attempt to read, searching the far corners of my brain for the high school French the nuns crammed in there somewhere. I've loved pretending to live here, pretending to be native to this southern coast, going to the market with my leather-handled straw basket, walking up the slant of a side street to take my French lesson from Mme Lecat who shakes her head, purses her lips as only the French can do, and says, *"Non . . . non, non, non."*

It is wonderfully bracing to be disapproved of by the French. You know you've been taken seriously, that life is affirmed as a serious matter of form, not simply a business of messy content. *Comme il faut, Patricia! Comme il faut!* And I do, suddenly, passionately, want to do things as they *should,* as they *must* be done.

The disapproval isn't personal. It is simply the way things must be. Do not eat a bouillabaisse whose ingredients have not been first presented to you on a platter, the fish still weakly leaping from the silver dish. Only buy bread from the Lion d'Or boulangerie on rue Victor Hugo. All restaurants on the port are tourist traps. And much, much more. Life is covered with a gilded template of right ways and wrong turns. These are the rules of Mme Lecat, and I cannot expect to improve my French if I am unwilling to learn this grammar as well. When we go to the market together she shakes her head as I turn to one sausage stand, and nods approvingly toward another. They look identical. But I am now incapable of going to the first sausage stand.

Tears squinted in my eyes when the cheese man at the market (Mme Lecat's cheese man, not the *other* one) said he would miss me. He came from behind his counter and took my hand. But the main thing about being here: how exactly it has been as I imagined it before I came. The little quais of this small Mediterranean harbor are crowded with family pleasure craft and a few, very few now, fishing boats, the air tangy with—what is it?—I want to say lavender but that may be from my own T-shirt that has been in a drawer I layered with sachets I bought at last week's market. Beyond the flowers and sea-foam, there is always a wake-up-and-smell-the-coffee smell coming from the cafés that ring and define the harbor, and brief puffs of gasoline from the delivery vans and Vespas that go by.

I've been here off-season, which makes Cassis and all the towns I've visited along the Riviera these past months seem old-fashioned because empty, the social world slow enough for conversation, for banter, for the sitting-and-staring that is the core of living: the *just looking* of the artist life. The rush that is modernity has been on vacation while I've been here, living in the slo-mo of off-season, a replica of times past. On the weekends things begin to get crowded now and my northern soul sniffs the warmth: summer is coming, and it's clear I must go. Soon this won't be my place anymore.

My saints, most of them, eventually left here, too. Mansfield decamped to the thin air of Switzerland where, for a while, she thought she could breathe better, then she moved on to her Russian guru and the feverish mystic hopes of her last consumptive months. Fitzgerald went, too—of course *not* back to St. Paul as I will soon do. "I never did quite adjust myself to those damn Minnesota winters," he wrote from Baltimore to an old St. Paul friend in 1934. "It was always freezing my cheeks, being a rotten skater . . . though many events there will always fill me with a tremendous nostalgia." But it was the grudging nostalgia of one still loyal to his early escape, and not only because of the weather. New York, the Riviera, the whole

sliver of the East Coast from Baltimore to New York—
these were his chosen places, the places of his success, not
his formation.

Jerome Hill, the St. Paul boy from the other end of
Summit Avenue, did stay in the French paradise, though
he lived as the rich do, in seasonal homes—a New York
apartment in winter, Cassis in summer, skiing and traveling here, there. Only Matisse remained entirely loyal to
the bliss of this place, the love-at-first-sight joy he experienced when, a working boy from the north, he found not
only himself but his subject in the light of the south and
intuited it would be his glory.

In 1918, early in the odalisque years, he was staying at
the Hôtel de la Mediterranée in Nice. Looking back years
later he still delighted in it, his memory full of exclama-
tion—"an old-fashioned hotel, of course! And how
lovely the ceilings in the Italian way! What tiled floors! . . .
I stayed there four years for the pleasure of painting nudes
and figures in an old rococo sitting room. Do you remember the light that came through the shutters? It came
from underneath, as if from the footlights. Everything
was false, absurd, splendid, delicious."

As if he required distance from sincerity and earnest-ness—the wearying northern virtues—in order to *get it.* Get the light, get the color. Accuracy and even truth could only be found in a stagecraft that was "false," "absurd." Beauty—yes, but nothing pretty. He sought the core ele-ments of the splendid, not because they were lovely but because they bespoke the longing at the core of a creature alive in a created world. He was, even in this, trying to "convey all his emotion," as he had said as a young man trying to understand the brilliance of Rembrandt's bibli-cal scenes. The authority of Rembrandt's paintings arose not from accuracy but from the shot arrow of perception piercing the living world. That was art, to be able to con-vey this transaction on the ground of its happening—that is, to express "all his emotion." To see in order to at-test to what *is.* To keep taking notes for "the celestial process" as Henry James called the work of making art.

A moment ago, as I was writing this, still trying, I sup-pose, to express all *my* emotion, a beautiful girl, jaunty and at the height of her self-certainty as a woman, drove by M. Brun's with breathtaking assurance on a little con-veyance, a sort of cart with an open driving seat, the kind of vehicle you might see on a golf course. The men sweeping the pavement before their shops paused, an unsighed sigh in their pause. She wore old jeans, poured down her endless legs. They hung by a breath from her hips, and a bright orange T-shirt winked at her midriff, exposing a band of golden skin—her flat stomach and the beginning of her slim hips. She was ferrying crates of oranges mounded up behind her on the toy cart to the fish restaurants around the port. I almost laughed out loud—a girl in orange, even a tincture of orange on her flawless, flaunted flesh, delivering oranges that are just coming in now from Italy. Or maybe they come from Algeria, straight across the water.

Sitting here, a person without any employment except *to look*, I have an uncanny sense that things here in this light, the world itself and all its haphazard parts, have a way of coming together to *form* something—sun, the lick of the morning air off the sea, shopkeepers leaning on big brooms, gulls sweeping the sky, the ruined medieval château on the crown of the bluff across the harbor almost effaced in the light, insubstantial but enduring like the past as it recedes and enriches itself in the mind.

This leisure offers up for the *just-looking* person café after café around this old port (even if it is a borrowed slowness, the leisure of travel and a few months' free time), old men walking, slightly bent, batons of bread under their arms like benign weapons. All of it arranges itself. Or the light arranges it.

Of course I've just described (and become) a stereotype—the ardent American tourist taking in what accords with her prearrival dream, a scene arranged for her consumption by willing tourism offices and shopkeepers (the coffee at M. Brun is for the tourists, Mme Lecat, a native Cassisdian, says with disdain. Don't spend your money there. In this alone I must disobey her). But what is the difference between a stereotype and this penetrating desire in the face of splendor, of what was long imagined in the cold north and came true in this glittering south?

THERE IS ONE MORE pilgrimage to make. From Marseille to Vence, the little town not far from Nice where Matisse lived from 1943 to 1946 in a villa called Le Rêve, "The Dream." On the insistence of his doctor who advised against the sea air of Nice, Matisse had been living above Nice in Cimiez at the Hotel Regina since 1938, exiled from his beloved view and the watery light of the Mediterranean. Still, he thought of the period that began in 1941 (and lasted until his death in 1954) as his "second life." He'd undergone a harrowing operation for duodenal cancer in 1941, followed by pulmonary embolisms and then flu. It was a miracle—he believed and everyone around him believed—that he was alive at all.

After an air raid on Cimiez, he moved for the rest of the war to Vence, where his long convalescence continued. Before he moved to Vence, while still an invalid in Cimiez, he met the woman who was to be his last great model, who, in her own second life became the unlikely muse who led him back to his beginnings for the last great work of his long life.

Just as Lydia Delectorskaya had first come into his household as a companion for Mme Matisse, and only some months later became Matisse's model after his "grim and penetrating stare" fastened on her, so this time the muse arrived as a nurse. Only the patient now was

Matisse, and the woman was a young nursing student. Her name was Monique Bourgeois. Her father had just died of his war wounds. She was recovering from a tubercular lung herself, was broke, unable to return yet to nursing school, and desperate for a job. A nursing service in Nice sent her to Cimiez to the famous Matisse (she had never heard of him), telling her that it was a temporary post—and she should not tell him she had only completed one year of nursing school. Matisse, she was told, was "looking for a young and pretty night nurse."

At twenty-one, Monique Bourgeois felt she qualified as young, but pretty? She had serious misgivings. But she needed the job.

"That was September 26, 1942," she writes in her memoir. "I rang the bell. A tall, blond young woman, with very pale skin, opened the door." This was Delectorskaya, by now the keeper of the house and the health of Matisse. Not simply a muse, but a kind of beloved disciple, an acolyte, wifely and secretarial. "He's a very important man," she told Monique, "you have to take the best possible care of him."

Into this invalid setting devoted not simply to the care of a very ill old man but even more essentially to sustaining his work as an artist, Monique Bourgeois came to change dressings and to see Matisse through the insomniac hours past midnight. She was the night nurse.

Sometime later he showed her some of his paintings and asked her opinion. "Monsieur," she said, "forgive me for saying this. I like the colors, but the shapes are just awful."

This of course delighted the Master. The hiccup of honesty, the charm of it after long years of fawning reverence. They became friends—as maybe is bound to happen to two people alone in the dead of night—between the warm milk, the therapeutic massage, the change of dressings. She read aloud to him but fell asleep, an exhausted child, and he told her to get some rest, turning into something of a night nurse himself. When he asked about her studies and she told him there was no money for her to resume them, he arranged for a scholarship. She told him he was a grandfather to her. He seems to have taken this to heart.

The regular night nurse returned, and Monique went to Vence to be with her family. Sometime later she received a telephone call from Cimiez. Matisse wanted her to pose for him. It was a job—and they had formed an attachment, a fondness and trust. She couldn't turn him down.

From these sessions Matisse painted a series of four stunning portraits of a woman in different gowns with plunging necklines, her regal head massed with a cascade of black curls. A beauty after all. One of them is titled *L'Idole,* the same title he had chosen for the portrait of his wife in 1906.

And then, after knowing Matisse a year and a half, working for him, posing for him, seeing him through the dark night, becoming part of his household, taken under the wing of this grandfather so soon after the loss of her own father, bound to him with the bonds of fondness and teasing honesty and the charmed and harmless flirtation that can arise between an old man and a young girl for whom the rules are clear and kept, Monique Bourgeois entered the Dominican convent at Monteils and became, to her patron's initial dismay, Sister Jacques-Marie. Like Matisse, she, too, had a calling.

WE HAVE COME from Marseille, a three-hour drive on the A-8 through Provence, to see the Chapel of the Rosary in Vence, the work Matisse did *for* Sister Jacques-Marie rather than *of* her as the portraits are. My old friend Michael, an American writer settled in Marseille, where he and his French wife live with their son, Noah, has agreed to drive me. He's always meant to visit the chapel, too. Jokes about the nice Jewish boy from Jersey who would make the perfect altar boy. More jokes about the Minnesota convent-school girl still going back to the nuns for more. We love to regale each other with our stock selves, the Old World stories of our old religions that put their mark on us early, the very selves we have tried to live and write ourselves out of, away from. And back to, back into. We argue over who has the more labyrinthine patterns of guilt—Jews or Catholics. We trade jokes—he tells the Catholic jokes, I tell the Jewish ones. The flowering landscape skims along outside the little car.

We think we're hilarious, topping each other with self-derision, betraying the odd affection the children of religion have for the faith that bedevils them, cracking the whip of humor. Isabelle, Michael's wife, laughs at us when we do this. She can't believe how serious Americans are about religion. She is beautiful and gentle, and doesn't take a razor to her "background," her "heritage," as her husband and I do to ours. Maybe that's because, living in Marseille, up the hill from that bronze plaque embedded in the Vieux Port, she has seen the civilizations come and go, radiating one set of gods after another, and somewhere in her prudent native-memory, she can't rise to the old bait.

But I can, I do. Still looking for love—that is, the sublime—in all the wrong places. As if the sea weren't enough, the bowl of coffee at M. Brun, the lavender fields, the cheese man at the market who took my hand. As if my love and life at home, waiting for me on Laurel Avenue in old St. Paul, were not enough. I have never succeeded in giving over wholly to the things of the earth, always reaching up. *Up*—the first word, I read in a biography, that Scott Fitzgerald said as a baby—reflecting that terrible urge to transcend that perhaps only death, that certain cheat, can finally satisfy.

But maybe this chapel will, after all, be "the place," the thing sought, the grail or the treasure—whatever it is that is supposed to be at the end of the rainbow of pilgrimage. Anyway, for now, I'm putting my faith—or at least my curiosity—in this great final effort by the master of the odalisque, the chapel whose making was prompted by the wish of a nun who had once been a fresh young girl, mourning her dead soldier father, a girl Matisse set before one of his mysterious screens and painted into a beautiful, commanding woman in a plunging neckline, her dark hair a glory.

WE'RE THE FIRST to enter the chapel when the volunteer (or nun? It's hard to tell who's a nun anymore) opens the gate for the afternoon hours. The chapel is white and unremarkable from the outside, modern and minimal. The brilliant blue roof is arresting, as is the thin, almost aerial cross with its surprising addition of Islamic-like crescents, glinting in the sun. There is a sly hint of a mosque to the place.

We wander through the small space, taking in the whole wall of stained glass leaves. The guidebook I buy at the museum shop explains that the design was taken from a passage from the Revelation of St. John referring to the tree of life "whose leaves were for the healing of the nations." A postwar peace chapel. The idea of the tree of life, I read, represents the Golden Age — not the one the ancients dreamed of, looking backward to a lost past, gazing at their goldfish in a bowl, the watery totems of that old dream. Rather, in the Christian way, abstract and wishful, it is the Golden Age to come, the Second Coming, the Return and Rapture. The colors are yellow, blue, green. And past the raised altar (chosen by Matisse because it looked like a cottage loaf of bread), another wall of stained glass, great desert leaves in yellow on a field of blue and green.

All the other walls are covered with white tiles, painted with the freehand strokes of the old man: The great wall-high Virgin holding her simple shape of a child is surrounded by flower-clouds, comical billows of good spirit.

The wall at the back, behind the small seating area, holds the Stations of the Cross, also black against the white tiles, but the hand here is not serene and playful, but pained, scratching its way to Golgotha.

Then, modestly placed in the corner at the back, as if not wishing to draw attention to itself is what I have come for: a small Moroccan door. I know immediately it is a confessional, the little room where you're supposed to tell the truth. Not simply your sins, I've always thought, but your truth. The rattle of wrongs, the bad moves, wrong turns, bum raps, false steps. The door is decorated with a wooden screen of intricate faux-Arabic script painted a glistening whipped-cream white, a faint mauve in the scrim behind the carving promising a different dimension beyond the closed surface. Open the door, open your heart. How I wanted to put my hand on it, and go there, Tell All.

Is that what was behind the screen that fascinated me all those years ago in Chicago—a confessional like the little box confessionals at St. Luke's? Standing stock-still in front of the woman gazing at the aquarium, the screen behind her (I remember it held a promise of aquamarine as this carved door promises lavender) beckoned me, seeming to promise something. I thought it was the whole exotic world "out there" or possibly "over there." The secret world of Real Life that I sensed I had not yet cracked with my English-major earnestness, my literary dreams, and my Midwestern flyover soul. But here it is again, like a second chance. And it proves to be a door—and not to somewhere else, but to something else. A door to a tiny room where you tell your truth and are forgiven.

I tell Michael I'm disappointed that the sign says there is Mass for the public only on Sundays. That's several days away when I'll be long gone. He scurries off with his perfect French and his easy charm and his journalist's assumptions, and returns smiling: we have been invited to attend Mass the following morning at 9:00 AM. Simply ring the bell at the convent next door, and enter through the garden. Oh, and by the way, Sister Jacques-Marie is here. She will be happy to sign your book—for I am clutching two copies of her memoir, one in French, one in English.

"She's *alive*?" I say incredulously.

"Very," the woman (nun? volunteer?) behind the counter says, smiling at my gaucherie.

SISTER JACQUES-MARIE, I decide, must be the tall, thin older woman (how old? Eighty? That would be about right) I am seated next to the next morning in the chapel. She has a brisk way about her and shows me where the service starts in the prayer book without looking at me, just taking my book and opening it. There aren't many nuns in this convent, it appears. Perhaps a dozen, and only one, very old, rather dumpy, wearing the habit. The others are dressed sensibly, their hair cut short, their bodies lithe and trim. Quick smiles, easy, graceful manners.

Michael has never been to a Mass before, but the younger nun who was organizing things spoke to him the day before and knew his French was good. She comes up now as we sit in a choir pew with the small congregation of a dozen nuns and asks him to do the first reading. A Jewish altar boy after all.

During Mass the light plays against the white tiles, slowly changing in what seems a profoundly subtle light show, the brilliant colors of the stained glass paying out the frailest pearl tones against the shimmering white. I stare—can't help staring—at the wall where the Virgin stands amidst her flower-clouds on the softly glowing tiles. I watch the light move. I almost forget I'm sitting next to Sister Jacques-Marie. I should be "observing" her, taking notes.

But in fact, it is the bent elderly nun, the dumpy one in full habit, wearing the Dominican white, her short veil revealing a small band of gray hair, who proves to be Sister Jacques-Marie. She needs help when she walks from the chapel to the convent. The younger nun points her out, and we rush from the chapel to intercept her.

Yes, she would be happy to sit and talk, she has some time. She asks me to take her arm. Or rather, she commandeers my arm. I feel her weight on me as she leads us to the convent. I would like to walk slowly in this convent garden with her for a long while. A bower of bliss, roses everywhere. But she takes us to a shadowy parlor with a large oval table where she sits down heavily, gripping the edge of the table. Clearly she is in pain, but her face is long used to smiling, a habit of wit has impressed itself in the

corners of her small dark eyes, deep in her oval face, a face
of only a few strokes, I thought. A Matisse face even now.

She signs my copy of her book: *For Patricia, in memory of
your stay at the Chapel of the Rosary. I hope that this book is "truth."*
The little shrug of the quotation marks implying a wry acknowledgment that truth, of all things, can't be counted
on, even with the best intentions of the writer.

Matisse liked women, she says, liked to have pretty
women around, draw them, paint them. She smiles happily at this fact, this memory. He was always correct with
me, of course, she says, in case I thought she meant something else, though there is nothing of the prude about
this remark. Apparently it is part of her *vérité.* She speaks
happily, not like a nervous virgin, but with the knowledge
of the nature of the love they had. *We were friends, we cared
for each other.*

And what of Lydia Delectorskaya? I ask. The faithful
muse of the long, late years, what became of her?

Ah, she committed suicide. Only a few years ago, as an
old woman.

Suicide? I'm genuinely shocked, not simply that she
killed herself but that she had lived so long.

I realize, looking at Soeur Jacques-Marie's old face, finely lined, burned by the sun (she had spent her life at a convent in Biarritz, far from the chapel she had inspired, working as an occupational therapist) that she is now about the age Matisse was when she came to him as a night nurse and won his heart.

It was very sad, she says then of Delectorskaya. Her face holds the thought of this sadness a moment, as if in loyalty. Then she shrugs again, accepting it, apparently.

IN THE CHAPEL my main task was to create an equilibrium between one surface that was filled with light and colour and the opposite wall which was relieved only by the line drawings in black on white. For me, the chapel meant the fulfillment of a whole life devoted to my work. It was the flowering of hard and difficult but honest labours.

Matisse considered the Chapel of the Rosary his masterwork, the culminating attempt—to achieve the essence and depth of blue he had sought all his life, and to respond to question after question he had been asking of line, color, surface, over his long years on canvas and paper. The chapel was his opera, the big theatrical, living work.

And it was a place of worship. A church made with ferocious attention to the detail and to the iconography of Christianity by a man who had long ago fled the Church and its dark and devious prohibitions, its powerful denials of the flesh he had devoted his best years to worshipping and rendering. The year the chapel was dedicated, 1951, Matisse responded to a series of interview questions from a writer named André Verdet who asked him if there was any part of his work he felt was misunderstood by critics.

The odalisques, he said, they had not been understood. "Did I paint too many Odalisques," he asked,

was I carried away by excessive enthusiasm in the happiness of creating those pictures, a happiness that swept me along like a warm ocean ground swell? I still don't know . . . I had to catch my breath, to relax and forget my worries, far from Paris. The Odalisques were the fruits of a happy nostalgia, of a lovely, lively dream and of the almost ecstatic, chanted experience of those days and nights, in the incantation of the Moroccan climate. I felt the irresistible need to express that ecstasy, that divine nonchalance, in corresponding colored rhythms, the rhythms of sunny and lavish figures and colors.

Divine nonchalance—that was it, the double aspect of his long passion coupled with his extraordinary discipline, the daily stroke of the brush, pull of the pencil. In all that nonchalance, the glory of ease, to experience the ecstasy that is our only sure link with divinity. No wonder there were all those lounging women in their complicated interiors, and he had the guilty sensation of perhaps painting "too many" of them, being incapable of moving past their languor. They aren't weary; they're necessarily careless, bred of the imagined ease of creativity even as their maker worked like a Trojan to accomplish their languor.

It takes time to do this, the cloistered nun said to me of her job all those years ago. This divine nonchalance, the leisure of great, private endeavor, was a grace that suffused all four of the plunging-neckline portraits of Monique Bourgeois. Matisse managed to rest the sacred ease of creation upon her image. A form of love, to be so at ease in the frantic world, to be so at peace in the presence of beauty.

And then, a true odalisque, his model, perhaps all his models, trumped him. She drew herself back, keeping her mystery to herself, even as the artist thinks he has it safely inscribed on canvas, as a writer thinks the truth of the ineffable can be lured onto the page.

The model rises. She discards the alluring costume, the bright yellow beads, the masquerade that was so necessary to beguile her truth to canvas. She leaves it all, she walks behind the cloister screen, into her own life, where she cannot be seen but only imagined. Maybe not even imagined—only longed for. It is a life he would not have chosen for her, a life he can only gaze on as she disappears into the blue backdrop of her own divine nonchalance.

ACKNOWLEDGMENTS

Personal essays belong to the amateur tradition, to the "common reader" as Virginia Woolf put it. In my case, the common viewer. Given this amateur status, I'm especially indebted to the scholarship of others, and in the bibliography have tried to note the works I have quoted from or that figured in my thinking. Pierre Schneider's magisterial study of Matisse was essential, and I'm particularly grateful to Hilary Spurling whose meticulous reconstructions have made the personal life and artistic process of Henri Matisse vividly available as never before. To Claire Tomalin whose work on Katherine Mansfield corrected narrower readings of her life I am most thankful as well.

I was greatly assisted by a residency at the Camargo Foundation in Cassis, France, originally the home of Jerome Hill, and established by him as a residence for scholars and artists. The University of Minnesota has generously supported my work and travel as a Regents Professor of English.

Generous friends and correspondents encouraged me, stood with me before paintings in museums as I scribbled in notebooks, challenged and corrected me along the way, and sometimes made possible essential travels and encounters. I remain grateful to them all: Mark Doty; Deborah Chasman; Helene Atwan; Rhoda Weyr; Carol Houck Smith; Sybil Kretzmer; Susan and Steffen Kyhl; Michael Blumenthal; Peter Day; Janet Landay; Lynn Freed; Eva Hoffman; Robert Zaretsky; Samuel Heins and Stacey Mills; Phebe Hanson; Mary Gordon, Deborah Garfinkle, and Nicola Beauman of Persephone Books; Linda Gregerson and Steven Mullaney; Burton Shapiro; Charles Sugnet; Charles Baxter; Thomas Mallon; Andrea Barrett; Edward Hirsch; Carol Conroy; Nancy Larson

Shapiro; Steven Sorman; Terrence Williams; Kate Martin, OSC; Judith Zinsser; Rosemarie Johnstone Weinstein; Eric Marty; Imi Hwangbo; B. J. Carpenter; Cynthia Gehrig of the Jerome Foundation; John W. Chapman of the Minnesota Historical Society; Lyndel King of the Weisman Art Museum; Stephen Williams; Jonathan Williams; Susan Jesenko and the late Mark Jesenko; Maureen McAvey; Robert Clark; my stalwart agent, Marly Rusoff; meticulous—and hilarious—Managing Editor David Hough; and my ingenious editor, Ann Patty.

BIBLIOGRAPHY

Aragon, Louis. *Henri Matisse: A Novel.* Translated by Jean
   Stewart. New York: Harcourt Brace Jovanovich, 1972.

Calasso, Roberto. *Literature and the Gods.* Translated by Tim
   Parks. New York: A. A. Knopf, 2001.

Cowart, Jack, et al., ed. *Matisse in Morocco: The Paintings and
   Drawings, 1912–1913.* Washington, DC: National Gallery
   of Art; New York: H. N. Abrams, 1990.

Cowart, Jack, and Dominique Fourcade. *Henri Matisse:
   The Early Years in Nice, 1916–1930.* Washington, DC:
   National Gallery of Art; New York: H. N. Abrams,
   1986.

Delektorskaya, Lydia. *With Apparent Ease—Henri Matisse: Paintings from 1935–1939.* Translated by Olga Tourkoff. Paris: A. Maeght, 1988.

Djebar, Assia. *Women of Algiers in Their Apartment.* Translated by Marjolijn de Jager. Charlottesville: University of Virginia, 1992.

Flaubert, Gustave. *Flaubert in Egypt: A Sensibility on Tour.* Translated and edited by Francis Steegmuller. Chicago: Academy Chicago, 1979.

Halsband, Robert. *The Life of Lady Mary Wortley Montagu.* Oxford: Clarendon Press, 1956.

Lemaire, Gérard-Georges. *The Orient in Western Art.* English ed. Cologne: Könemann Verlagsgesellschaft, 2001.

Matisse, Henri. *Matisse on Art.* Edited by Jack Flam. Rev. ed. The Documents of Twentieth-Century Art. Berkeley: University of California Press, 1995.

Russell, John. *Matisse: Father and Son.* New York: H. N. Abrams, 1999.

Said, Edward W. *Orientalism.* 25th anniversary ed. New York: Vintage Books, 1994.

Schneider, Pierre. *Matisse.* New York: Rizzoli, 2002.

Spurling, Hilary. *Matisse the Master: A Life of Henri Matisse, The Conquest of Color, 1909–1954.* New York: A. A. Knopf, 2005.

—————. *The Unknown Matisse: A Life of Henri Matisse, The Early Years, 1869–1908.* London: Hamish Hamilton, 1998.

Yeazell, Ruth Bernard. *Harems of the Mind: Passages of Western Art and Literature.* New Haven: Yale University Press, 2000.